Community and the Soul of Ireland

Community and the Soul of Ireland

The Need for Values-Based Change

A Conversation with Fr Harry Bohan

with Frank Shouldice

The Liffey Press
Dublin

Published by The Liffey Press
Ashbrook House, 10 Main Street,
Raheny, Dublin 5, Ireland
www.theliffeypress.com

A catalogue record of this book is
available from the British Library.

ISBN 1-904148-22-0

Printed in the Republic of Ireland by Colour Books Ltd.

Contents

About Fr Harry Bohan
and the Céifin Institute

Fr Harry Bohan was born in 1938 in Feakle, County Clare. The son of a publican, he was educated at the local national school and St Flannan's College in Ennis before attending Maynooth College, where he was ordained in 1963.

Under the tutelage of Dr Jeremiah Newman, he developed a keen interest in rural sociology and resumed his studies at the University of South Wales, Cardiff, graduating with an M.Sc.Econ after completing his Masters thesis on "The Effects of Industrialisation on the Settlement Patterns of Britain".

He worked with the Irish community in Birmingham before returning to Ireland in 1968. In an attempt to stem mass emigration from his native county, he founded the Rural Housing Organisation in 1972, seeking to preserve and develop local rural communities throughout the west of Ireland.

Fully resettled in his native County Clare, Fr Bohan got heavily involved in the GAA, renewing a childhood love for hurling by taking up management of the county hurling team. He led Clare to consecutive National League titles in 1977 and 1978.

The Rural Housing Organisation became the Rural Resource Organisation in 1983, expanding its role into employment programmes and resource development. The organisation's objectives were informed by awareness of a rural/urban dynamic in Irish society.

The RRO further broadened its activities by setting up Rural Finance and Rural Resource Centre, both linking into development programmes to counter local unemployment and emigration.

In partnership with other organisations, the RRO has since merged into the Rural Resource Development (RRD), based in Shannon. With Fr Bohan as director, the RRD has presided over strong economic progress in the region, en-suring that the west of Ireland achieved its share of phe-nomenal national growth during the so-called Celtic Tiger era. By 1997, he began to look beyond the rural/urban dy-namic and explore the global/local dimension of change.

A three-day RRD conference in 1998 ("Are We Forget-ting Something?") examined how the balance of daily life had been disturbed by the upsurge in economic activity. A huge response to that debate prompted further conferences each year to discuss diverse aspects of social and economic development.

The conferences also copper-fastened the formation of the Céifin Institute — the name derives from Céibhfhionn, the Celtic Goddess of Inspiration.

Initially responding to issues raised by its annual confer-ences, the purpose of Céifin is to reflect, debate and direct values-led change in Irish society.

Fr Bohan sees Céifin developing into a national move-ment with regional branches and locally based networks backed up by extensive academic studies. Pending approval for building costs, the Céifin Institute will be located at a 39-acre site in Newmarket-on-Fergus, County Clare.

Fr Bohan is a priest in the diocese of Killaloe. He has spoken extensively on issues of Christianity and economic development. He has published on the theme in *Ireland Green* (1979), *Roots in a Changing Society* (1982) and *Hope Begins At Home* (1993). He is also co-editor and contributor to *Are We Forgetting Something?*, *Working Towards Balance*, *Re-defining Roles and Relationships* and *Is the Future My Responsibility?*

For further information, contact:

The Céifin Centre
Town Hall, Shannon, Co. Clare, Ireland
Tel: +353 (0)61 365912
E-mail: ceifin@eircom.net
Website: www.ceifin.com

About the Interviewer

Dubliner Frank Shouldice is a journalist, playwright and television director. He has written for all the national newspapers in Ireland. He wrote a weekly column for *Ireland on Sunday* from 1997–99, prior to which he was Associate Editor of the *Irish Voice* in New York. He worked as producer/director with *The Soccer Show* on RTE and also directed *Breaking Ball*, the popular GAA TV series for Setanta Productions. Frank has also written and directed numerous plays for stage, including *TráWatch* and *Marie Clare*. His last play *Journeyman* has been staged in Dublin, Belfast and Glasgow, and he also adapted the play for RTE Radio's *Play Date*.

Preface

Two weeks after holding an extended interview with Fr Harry Bohan in Shannon, an articulated truck landed in the River Liffey in Dublin. Fr Harry was not actually driving the truck but somehow both events seemed inextricably connected.

Fr Harry had been articulating concerns about the direction Irish society is taking. In our headlong rush through economic success, he feels we ignore the alarm bells ringing loudly on deficits in human spirituality, our quality of life, a confusion of priorities and a hollow charge towards unattainable fulfilment.

The northbound truck was also in a headlong rush but obviously to a less philosophical conclusion.

Fr Harry portrays a troubled scenario which seems to pass us by, almost unnoticed. The more he speaks about it, the more familiar his observations become. The range of his analysis leaves no stone unturned and the more you consider his position the more convincingly it applies across the board.

Long before he pauses for breath, you begin to see modernity extend a finger or two in every direction. Many of these changes have been ushered through as a sign of society advancing, sweeping away the old and ringing in the new. Despite widespread concern about how this transition is being handled, objections are largely muted for fear of standing in the way of progress. Or being branded for doing so.

We've been through the hard times, so our collective impulse is to grab what's going. Impulses, however, aren't built for the long haul.

Indeed, the pace of life may be slower, quieter and gentler in Shannon, but at the end of our discussion with Fr Harry, publisher David Givens and I found ourselves caught in a rush-hour traffic jam lodged like a wet snail between Limerick and Ennis. The global village had gone west and suddenly Dublin did not seem so far away.

Reading through Fr Harry's earlier work, it is equally striking that he has seen the changes coming for some time now. His message over the years is consistent and clear. Social concerns may drive his economic theory, but it is important to him that these theories make sense. If they don't add up, he will try a fresh approach until the underlying problems are squarely addressed.

The dynamics of the Liffey crash are simple enough. The truck and trailer — a powerful 24-wheel unit — collided with a delivery truck at the intersection of Tara Street and Burgh Quay in Dublin's city centre. The truck and trailer veered right and crashed through the stone ramparts of Butt Bridge, its momentum taking it over the precipice and dropping into the water below.

Fortunately for the driver, the tide was low, thus turning the headlines from "Horrific Disaster" into "Lucky Escape!" A fireman from nearby Tara Street station swam to the cab and the driver, although shaken, was helped to safety.

Once the sturdy old bridge was declared structurally safe, rush-hour morning traffic funnelled past the crash site in a single-lane crawl. Three high cranes were deployed to remove the vehicle and restore the Liffey to its less than pristine condition.

The stress levels of passing motorists was momentarily distracted by the spectacular sight of a juggernaut jack-knifed in the Liffey. Like most people who witness accident or tragedy, the visual shock is tempered, however briefly, by the thought, "That could have been me".

You might think I am making a bit much out of a random accident. The point is, we should question whether this peculiar set of circumstances is quite so random.

A couple of months after the Dublin collision, another juggernaut hit a bridge over the Boyne River at Slane. It could have been another random incident, except it was the third serious truck crash at the bridge in two years.

Might our way of life have something to do with such events that unfold before us with increasing regularity? Would these things happen if the system was not creaking at the seams?

More high-performance cars are sold in Ireland these days than at any period in the history of the state. People might buy the dream on wheels but even top-of-the-range models can't take you out of the real world. Last year, over 300,000 speeding fines were issued, while more than 400 people were killed on the roads. Yet at a time when the uninsured can't get a hospital bed, the state has allocated over €1 billion for road construction this year alone.

Consumption is even more conspicuous on faster getaway items like alcohol and drugs, or return tickets via addiction therapy or counselling services. By coincidence — or perhaps not — the World Wealth Report of New York notes that there are now 15,000 millionaires in the Republic of Ireland. Translated into one millionaire for every 253 citizens, you would think there's plenty to go round. Not so.

A study this year by the UN Development Programme concluded that Irish society has the highest level of poverty in the western world outside the US. The gap, everwidening, between rich and poor underlines deep inequalities within Irish society. Predictably, the government response in Dublin was to dismiss the study as out-of-date. The reality of everyday life, however, suggests the UN report will hold true for years to come.

Standard indices suggest we're going through a very difficult period of social change. As Fr Harry points out, traditionally powerful institutions have been unable to deal with such a rapid transition. Maybe problems in our society are exacerbated by prosperity arriving so suddenly or the uneven distribution of that wealth. Either way, many of the changes are hardly for the better.

And we're not just talking about juggernauts crashing. Marital breakdown also reflects growing tensions in our society — since legislation was passed in 1997, the divorce rate runs at about 2,500 cases annually. The national suicide rate, particularly among young males, has also increased exponentially, as has homelessness, street violence and the incidence of sex-related crime.

Officials elected to national office are routinely facing charges of corruption. Ireland's new ethnic diversity has exceeded the country's capacity to absorb it; the traditional non-conformity of travellers to settled life sustains mutual distrust and intolerance; patients in casualty wards are left overnight on trolleys in hospital corridors; while beach, river and lake resorts all over the country have been placed off-limits due to pollution.

If we stand back to consider the age we live in, we might find a society in which minorities, the poor and the vulnerable, the aged and the sick, are increasingly cast aside in the name of progress. It will hardly surprise us that the environment, for so long cherished as a natural resource in Ireland, has not fared any better. Might anybody other than Fr Harry begin to think we're already heading off course? The response to conferences set up by the Céifin Institute suggests that many others feel the same way. A vigorous debate has opened around the values that are shaping society. There is not just an awareness of what is going on but a growing realisation that ordinary people can — and must — do something about it. One of the most telling remarks Fr Harry makes is when he recalls a successful company executive stepping up to bat for change. And why? Because he doesn't like the Ireland his children are inheriting.

Céifin has the potential to become a popular movement, empowering Irish people to rebuild society from the ground up, create new models of community and bring balance to their lives. Fr Harry is a capable and willing steward in this process.

There is a crossover here to the thinking of the late John Healy, a fine political journalist from Ballaghadereen, County Roscommon. Healy became a strong voice decrying the gradual erosion of life in the west of Ireland, the loss of people, values, life and although he became closely associated with Fianna Fáil, Healy spoke passionately about the dearth of official action to stop the rot.

His writings found full expression in two memorable books — *Death of an Irish Town: No One Shouted Stop* and *Nineteen Acres*, the epilogue of which began, "This has not been an easy book to write: it may not be an easy book for my family to live with at first but in the end I hope they will come to appreciate what it is I have tried to do and say; not only about my mother's family, but for all the families like hers whose struggle, just to exist, is part of the story of modern Ireland."

This, in contrast, has been an uncomfortably easy book to write. Fr Harry's misgivings about Ireland's present course now echo John Healy's concerns about the plight of the West in the 1970s. Both are shouting stop but neither can tell if anybody is listening. Both wonder if change is happening so quickly that we hardly notice it any more. Both may be right.

*   *   *

Trends aren't random. Seven months before the juggernaut crash in Dublin, an express bus smashed through the bridge *at precisely the same point* — the southwest corner of Butt Bridge — and ended up in the Liffey.

It was a dark, cold December night and the river's waters submerged the cab end of the bus where the driver lay unconscious. A Scottish passer-by, Dimitrios Paraskevakis ran to the scene. A homeless man, Tony Paget, joined Paraskevakis at the river bank.

Ignoring all personal risk, the two men jumped into the freezing water and hauled the driver to safety. Injured passengers were taken away by ambulance and the rescuers were given a blanket to dry off. A crane removed the bus and within hours everything returned to normal.

Dimitrios Paraskevakis went home. Tony Paget reclaimed the cold spot on city concrete that served as his bed. He attempted to dry out his clothes and shivered through the wintry night. By daybreak, the media proclaimed him a national hero.

Several months later, Paraskevakis and Paget were honoured for their courage. They received medals from Irish Water Safety's "Just In Time" award. On the morning of the award ceremony Tony Paget's accommodation was a laneway off Moore Street. He was still homeless and even in the boom times his distinguished action failed to improve his situation, or that of some 5,000 people like him who inhabit a capital city infatuated with success.

Instead, he was given a medal, an *hors d'oeuvre* and a clap on the back before being allowed return to the abandoned car he called home. As an earlier Céifin conference asked, *are we missing something?*

Perhaps it's hugely symbolic that the articulated truck crashed through the very same wall as the express bus. But does anybody see past the symbolism of events happening before our eyes? Are these warnings to be ignored?

These are questions that Fr Harry and the Céifin Institute are asking. Critical issues relate to almost every facet — the post-Celtic Tiger phase — of our fast-changing history. Fr Harry's passion on these matters is apparent to anybody who has met him, driven by the same ethos which underpinned his work with the rural-development schemes.

These schemes, which changed the world for over 2,500 families, were undertaken against all expert advice. History shows the experts were wrong and the means justified the ends. Back then, as now, he attempts to match what is needed with what will work. The next step is to make that happen.

Against a backdrop of infrequently asked questions, Céifin's academic thrust makes perfect sense. As a society, we seem unsure as to how we have arrived where we are. Put it down to Fr Harry's sociological training but understanding the past will offer theoretical rigour to planning for the future. The approach he takes is practical and relevant. Lightning, it appears, can actually strike twice but if we stand back from where we are we might be able to figure out where we're going.

Butt Bridge does not look so well these days. Traffic descends on it at speed from perpendicular angles at Tara Street and Burgh Quay. Fly-by motorists frequently miss each other on the change of a light that leaves seconds to spare.

Further up the quays, at the intersection of Westmoreland Street and Aston Quay, withering flowers mark spots where pedestrians and cyclists were fatally injured in daylight hours. The answer provided by civic authorities was to erect a clock which counts down the seconds to the next crossing opportunity.

Time, it seems, is in decreasing supply. Everything is a race. Harried, stressed-out people vie for a toehold on the pavement, ready to swarm across in numbers at the wrong moment. The warning bells, as Fr Harry says, are ringing loudly, as loudly as the next batch of high-powered engines revving under a red traffic light. No one stopped when John Healy raised his hand forty years ago. The noise has got louder but if we continue to ignore it, we will end up drawing straws to cross the road.

In this book, Fr Harry is shouting stop. It is our time to listen.

Frank Shouldice
Dublin, August 2002

Part One

The Lost Generation

Frank Shouldice: *Four years ago, Céifin staged its first conference in Ennis which ran under the title "Are We Forgetting Something?" The conference generated energy, ideas and a lot of interest but significantly, when we talked about it, the first thing you mentioned was a chance remark made by a woman afterwards. Can you recall that conversation with her?*

Fr Harry Bohan: I remember it clearly. The conference had finished and people began breaking off into small groups, gathering in the hotel reception area and corridors outside the ballroom. I was talking to these people and I asked a woman what she got from the conference. She said, "Well, who's going to rear the next generation?" It was a question that stuck in my mind.

We chatted for a while about major changes that have come so quickly in work and family life in Ireland. How everybody seems to be rushing around and constantly feeling they haven't the time for anything. The modern way of life is challenging people's ability to achieve balance and, as this woman pointed out, the well-being of children is an issue of growing concern.

People are also beginning to see traditional institutions and support systems fall away and there's a degree of fear and uncertainty about what lies ahead of us. The pressures to make money are cutting into quality time we have for family and friends and even quiet time for ourselves.

I suppose the woman's remark underlined the fact that Ireland has obviously experienced an extraordinary transformation. The wider aspect of that change is how the country has become part of the globalised, capitalised world with an emphasis on the market economy and market values. In many ways she was suggesting that these values had taken over with very little emphasis on the values that shape life and give meaning to life.

FS: *Fair enough, but she's hardly the first parent to worry about her children. Why do you think that remark stayed with you?*

HB: I think what she was saying is something all of us feel — that change has come so extraordinarily fast that it's almost impossible to understand it. The whole point of that conference was to stand back and try to grasp the kind of changes that were taking place and to identify some issues that were central to that change.

When she asked that question, she was pointing out how we have become a very work-friendly society but not family-friendly. But she was also touching into the disconnecting of people generally from institutions of all kinds — family, community, church, state — and how the world of the marketplace, or the world of money, had become central to people's lives.

FS: *Arguably, each — or all — of these developments also had a positive impact on our changing times. Ireland did experience decades of mass emigration and high unemployment, from the 1950s and through the '70s and '80s. Should we also remind ourselves of that?*

HB: There is no question that a considerable amount of change has been very good. In a way I see this as a given. We had huge benefits in the 1990s, the standard of living improved and young people no longer had to emigrate.

It's hard to believe this island sent thousands of its youngest and brightest away each year through the 1950s and now, in a very short period of time, we have Irish people coming home from abroad as well as other nationals moving here. It's a remarkable transformation which underlines an economic potential that was not here, or certainly not harnessed, before.

So yes, there are enormous improvements. People have benefited, there's no question. What makes it interesting for us is how it happened so differently here than in other countries. In a way, the boom came so late to Ireland it gives us a great opportunity to look at the other side of economic growth and to restore a spiritual balance. That's actually where we are now.

FS: *If we are materially better off and school-leavers are no longer forced abroad in search of work, where's the problem?*

HB: These very positive developments have been accompanied by a change of — even a loss of — direction in ordinary human life. At times Irish society seems to be swamped by the worst aspects of global market culture and there's little understanding of the effect this has had on ordinary people.

The march towards economic and technological progress has cost us. There's been a social fallout that we tend to paper over or ignore. I think people are very confused because of the power of the market economy. It's about free movement of this and that but it's also about selling goods and selling entertainment. That's what it's about. We need to move on to other matters because of the impact the market has on society generally. The question now is, Who cares? We need to see ourselves and our neighbours as more than possible customers or fellow consumers.

FS: *So, who cares?*

HB: Actually a lot of people care because everyday events are bringing home to them that they need to care. We see other signs of this at Céifin, whether it's by the size of the attendance at our conferences, the demand for regional branches or the number of invitations we get to address interested groups. I really believe Irish people want to address what is happening.

FS: *Why were we so unprepared for these changes?*

HB: Because they came to us in one generation. In other western countries, this sort of transformation occurred over several generations. Social change has been more radical in Ireland, making it more difficult to cope.

The economic turnaround is a familiar story at this stage but my feeling is that it's actually been more difficult for us to cope with prosperity than it has been for previous generations to cope with poverty.

Collective success can be a burden when it changes our priorities, values and goals. New cultural patterns emerge. Relationships break down. We can feel so independent that we believe we no longer need others anymore. We can lose touch with the lived experience of others around us.

FS: *Is there a danger we are looking back on the past as the poor-but-happy old days? In reality it was, for many people, a time of genuine hardship and struggle.*

HB: I don't think there's any danger of romanticising the past. I lived through it myself and all over towns and villages in Clare — and all over the west — there was a drain of young people, skilled people, businesses and schools closing down. Through the 1950s you had 40,000 people leaving the country every year — and twice that decade it rose to 60,000 people emigrating.

Of course, we can draw lessons from the past but things have changed radically and we have to deal with the present. The search for human meaning and well-being is all around us. It's clear as day.

It is worth pointing out that even through days of mass unemployment and emigration, the role of the family was clear, that parental influence was strong and children had very tangible role models. People were involved from an early age in necessary work which gave us a sense of re-sponsibility and a sense of worth. There was more sharing across generations and because work opportunities were so limited, parents thought more about their children's future *character* rather than prospective *careers*.

It was a very vivid experience for me personally. I left primary school during that decade and watching so many of my school mates leave brought home to me the terrible reality of them having to go.

I mean, we grew up in Feakle and as kids we all thought the village would be our world and things would never change. I know that's a romantic, childish view but there's a difference when change is forced on you like it was on us.

There were 14 in our class. Nine had to emigrate. Within a few years of us finishing primary school, all of us were gone from the parish.

FS: *Was it easier to accept this as your "lot" if every kid in Feakle was in the same boat?*

HB: It wasn't easy to accept at all, because we didn't want to leave. I remember one morning seeing a girl from my class standing at the bridge in the middle of the village. She was standing there with her suitcase waiting for the bus. The bus would take her to Limerick and from there onto Cobh on her way to America. That meant she was going forever.

Even at that time I pledged I would do whatever I could to help people stay where they wanted to be. Change enforced like that was savage and this, more than anything else, inspired me to do something about it.

FS: *What happened to that girl?*

HB: I don't know. I never saw her again.

FS: *Writing a paper recently, you quoted Robert Kennedy extensively from a speech he made in 1968. Ireland in the '50s and the United States in the '60s were two very different places but you argue that the social fabric of both countries was stretched in the same direction.*

HB: Yes, because in Ireland the scourge of emigration brought about the breakdown of tight-knit communities and families. In America, the '60s brought huge, positive economic and social change but also marked a stripping down of what had been a rich community ethos.
In that speech, Robert Kennedy said:

> "Even if we act to erase material poverty, there is another great task. It is to confront the *poverty of satisfaction* — a lack of purpose and dignity — that inflicts us all. Too much and for too long we seem to have surrendered community excellence and community values in the mere accumulation of material things . . . . Gross National Product does not allow for the health of our children, the quality of their education or the joy of their play. It does not include the beauty of our poetry or the strength of our marriages; the intelligence of our public debate or the integrity of our officials. It measures neither our wit nor our courage; neither our wisdom nor our learning; neither our compassion nor our devotion to our country; it measures everything, in short, except that which makes life worthwhile."

I think there's something in that for us today. Events are telling us something has gone seriously wrong.

FS: *Could it be just a phase we're going through, the storm after the calm?*

HB: No, I think its part of a process that we're not managing very well. We need to be looking critically at the direction we're taking. And we need to start doing something about it.

It would be difficult to exaggerate the moral confusions of our day. We have to recognise the urgency and importance of finding an agreed basis for our conduct towards one another as sharers of life on this planet.

Schumacher once said it's not preachers and teachers who will get the message across; it's events. And the events are out there. They're screaming at us. There is certainly no shortage of events to warn us and in some cases, frighten us. Sometimes I wonder if we have become deaf to the sound of alarm bells ringing.

FS: *Your academic background is sociology. What aspect of the science were you drawn to?*

HB: The emigrant experience from my childhood in Feakle left a deep mark on me and I think that was what sent me looking in a particular direction. Even when I went to the seminary in Maynooth, I was very interested in the social encyclicals and what the Church's teaching was on these issues.

I completed a Masters degree in Cardiff on "The Effects of Industrialisation on the Settlement Patterns of Britain" and actually when I was working there I discovered an Irish community that had settled in Cardiff after the Famine.

I thought it was very interesting how conscious these people were of their past. This was generations after the first waves had arrived and yet they held onto that sense of origin. You'd find, for example, that they'd always cheer for Ireland at rugby internationals in Cardiff Arms Park.

FS: *The idea of making a home from home is a recurring theme for emigrants everywhere. Irish people often seem reluctant to simply adopt the social mores of the place they land, trying some-*

times to maintain a separate cultural existence. Do you think that
leads to particular tensions?

HB: Well, your identity is part of what you are and I think
in Ireland we are hugely aware of that. I often think of a
situation that arose in Birmingham. I got a phone call about a
case of domestic violence — the husband had beaten his
wife — and I went down to see them. These were Irish emigrants of that era, the couple and their five children. All
seven of them lived in a one-room flat with a bed on one
side of the room and the cooker in the other corner.

The woman was very upset and the man was ashamed of
what he had done. I remember when the situation had
calmed down a bit, the man said he was very sorry for hit-
ting his wife and he made no excuses for it. He said it wasn't
easy for them living as they were and that things might have
been different if they hadn't had to leave Ireland.

FS: *Maybe it would have happened anyway?*

HB: Maybe it would — I don't know — but I do feel the
conditions in which they lived were certainly a factor. It's
not to say there was no domestic violence in Ireland at the
time; I just mean that this couple were wrenched out of a
home environment and landed in strange territory. The man
could not cope.

These situations in overcrowded urban areas really
made a big impression on me and along with what I'd seen
growing up in Feakle set me against people having to leave
home against their will.

A few years after coming home, I founded the Rural
Housing Organisation (RHO) in 1972. I was concerned

about emigration from country areas and the effect it was having throughout the west of Ireland. People needed to be given an opportunity to stay. Affordable housing. The model has proven itself and since we set it up 30 years ago we've secured accommodation for over 2,500 families in 120 rural communities around the country.

After a while we expanded our interest into broader issues and the RHO became the Rural Resource Organisation in 1983.

FS: *Within a decade, Ireland had become a different place.*

HB: It really did. And since that period, the extent and pace of change has been phenomenal in so many areas — economic, religious and education. The main change was in employment. Certainly in the 1990s we were experiencing an economic miracle.

Of course, this was hugely welcome for a small island on the edge of Europe. The country had experienced famine and its aftermath, had tried to find its feet after independence and for decades had depended on emigration as a safety valve.

Putting bread on the table was always a priority for most Irish people. The 1990s offered us luxuries we never dreamed of. It was understandable — even natural — that the generation to experience this sudden prosperity would be sorely tempted to think of nothing else. And so we find ourselves, as a society, off balance.

Against this background, a few of us moved away from the rural/urban issue to look at the real issue of local/global. In the context of a market economy, how were we going to cope in our relationships and in making sense out of life?

What direction are we taking? What are our core values? What kind of people are we becoming?

FS: *Where do you find sociologists articulating what you find on the ground in your pastoral work?*

HB: There are a lot of critiques of modern society and to be honest I find most of them quite dull. They don't tell you anything new and tend to be fairly repetitive. Of course, there are others I have great respect for and I recently read something by Peter Abbott, a young English-born writer. He's a Cambridge graduate in his 20s and he wrote a piece that placed where his generation lies at the moment. When I was reading it, I thought it expressed the very ideas that brought Céifin about and what we stand for. It's an honest, perceptive account that gets to the heart of issues like alienation and "disconnectedness".

For example, he wrote,

> "I strongly believe . . . that the majority of young people are simply not attuned to discussing substantial and meaningful ideas. Young people don't like to be forced to think, they prefer entertainment handed to them on a plate and, unfortunately, this is what they are getting.

> "My generation is uniquely poised to assume stewardship of our planet. Like no other turning point in history, the dawn of the 21st century presents such immense challenges and opportunities that failure to live up to them could have potentially catastrophic consequences. If we do not start thinking, do not start beginning to be critical of the world around us and do not start to be genuinely discerning of popu-

lar culture then our world, and the world of our children, will surely reap the effects.

"But why are young people not thinking? Why are we not as actively involved in taking responsibility for our thoughts and actions? Why do we not perceive ourselves as being ready to assume responsibility for our planet and our neighbours? We recognise what needs to be done, yet we shirk from doing it. We complain too much, yet fail to offer solutions. Why is this?"

These are the sort of questions I find myself asking about society.

FS: *You're obviously singing from the same hymn sheet.*

HB: Without a doubt! I'm not quite in my twenties these days but there is a willingness to confront the issues here that I find very heartening.

He went on to examine the loss of faith in political systems and the loss of power of religious traditions. He describes the failure of leaders to focus on the big picture and tackle the *real* problems we are facing. He's spot-on there, because this is something I've watched happen and spoken out against for years.

Now that we have freedom, we need to take responsibility more than ever. People have to get involved, that's becoming increasingly obvious. This cuts across the board — whether it's parental, corporate, community, teacher, religious, professions, youth, political and public sector. Everybody is responsible.

If we're going to come up with new models of society we have to move away from this habit of compartmentalis-

ing people by sex, marital status, age, job, whatever. People
have to work together. And if we're going to assume responsibility, it's time for courageous, ethical, inspirational
leadership.

FS: *But how do you support the contention that the younger
generation does not think for itself?*

HB: Well, I'd agree with Abbott's claims that young people
recognise what's wrong. That's not the problem. But moving
towards a solution and taking responsibility for it is another
matter. As he wrote somewhere else, "Perhaps it is because
the problems can often seem so vast and intractable that we
feel powerless to effect any significant change."

That's probably true. So if we're going to address that
we have to empower people to effect change.

FS: *At one stage, you wrote, "There is a war going on for the
hearts and minds of young people." Is that an exaggerated way
to describe generational change?*

HB: No, because we can't get away from the fact that the
western world is being dictated and shaped by market values. A commercial world. People have a lot of things to sell
within that world and obviously mass advertising is at the
heart of that. Goods are sold in a very sophisticated way.
There's huge investment in marketing to win over the hearts
and minds of people, particularly young people.

The world of market values is so powerful because it
promises instant happiness and I think that's where difficulties arise. Massive resources are put into winning over
hearts and minds but while the methods are sophisticated,
the motivation is simple — to turn people into consumers.

What's being sold is the idea that there's a feelgood world out there waiting for them. All they have to do is buy it. A lot of that has to do with instant happiness, instant comfort and so on, whereas, for me, life isn't like that. Older people who have experienced life are aware of that.

Soul and spirit have to be fostered and nurtured to restore balance to our lives; we need to be connected with our inner selves, with others, with creation and with our Creator.

Any psychologist who has looked deep into the human mind and the human soul will say instant satisfaction does not give lasting happiness. Events are bringing home to us that there is a "war" out there.

FS: *Why do you think phenomena like the suicide rate or alcoholism or drug dependency have risen so significantly in Ireland?*

HB: I put it down to the fact that the social support system we had in poorer times was better adapted than the support system we've ended up with. In coping with poverty, there were some very powerful systems in place, particularly around family and community. These held people together. People shared their time, thoughts, stories, talents. They worked together, whereas now we have been disconnected from one another. There's a lot of loneliness and alone-ness. None of that is being addressed.

People have come to a level of disillusionment that's made them vulnerable in all kinds of ways. Suicide has risen by about 80 per cent since 1987. People come to the realisation that money can't buy everything. I think young people who have accumulated so much are discovering they can't buy meaning to life.

Secondly, look at the level of disillusionment among old people who are discovering serious flaws in the institutions they lived under. They too feel betrayed by these institutions.

Through our conferences, we hear so many young people saying we lack an identity. That sense — a lack of belonging — is becoming clear. We can't dream dreams any more because we have everything.

FS: *People had more serious problems in the past than not being able to dream. Besides, most dreams were unattainable back then. If socioeconomic change happened so quickly, we should be able to remember "not having". Why should it be so difficult to "have"?*

HB: I think it boils down to the human fact that people need people. There's a need to share but that need is getting sidelined by false "needs". And the gap between the two is creating deep-seated problems.

FS: *Few would disagree there's a trend towards individualism but this type of anonymity has also brought freedom and opportunity to break from social pressures and convention.*

HB: Okay, well let's say there's a new emphasis on self-interest. That has certain advantages and I would be the first to acknowledge the strength in people being self-confident and able to act from their own conviction. The thing is, a lot of people are finding it difficult to cope alone. That's what we're hearing and I think that's the key.

So if you take it back a little: Who cares? I would argue that a lot of people care but we need to understand what is going on and what we can do about it.

By extension, it raises other major questions. If self-interest is so dominant, other values become very critical — like honesty, truth, how we share the planet with one another. I suppose all these issues have been raised in Ireland over the last five, ten years.

I believe we've reached a point where we're looking at nothing short of a reconstruction of society built on trust. A lot of people want to re-direct the way things are heading but they don't know how to go about it, particularly because of massive change brought about by a booming economy and the decline of the institutions that used to write the script.

FS: *Would you feel it's easier to reconstruct the economy than to reconstruct society?*

HB: That's exactly it. Having constructed the economy we now have in place, how do we reconstruct society? People are now asking, how do we restore the balance. I think that's a fundamental question. Many commentators will say we have a global economy but not a global society and that's the way I'd see it too.

FS: *But how does this relate to everyday life?*

HB: Let me spell this out. It's in the daily newspaper or when you switch on the morning radio. Today, for example, the main news stories are about two murders committed in different parts of the country last night. That's happening practically every day. The fact that so many young lives can be destroyed by drug abuse. I'm hearing more and more young people saying, Who cares? Is that the kind of society we have created for them to grow up in?

I think they are challenging us now on the society they've grown into. It's the society of adults. I think that's very significant because when you consider all the scandals that have recently hit the surface; it wasn't young people who betrayed adults, it was adults who betrayed young people. It's not surprising there's a war going on for the minds and hearts of young people.

FS: *Do you mean that, when the good times came, we, as adults, took the money and ran?*

HB: To an extent, yes. If we look further, this is a society we have created without any critical examination. We need to look at it closely because the values in society to which we give priority affect every part of life.

I mean, we could pick an area — say education — and consider how it has been affected by these developments. For example, at Céifin we've started a study on the relationship between a school and its community. It deals with things like sense of place, sense of people, the social value of the school to its environs.

What we're finding is that people aren't used to looking at schools that way. We are conditioned all the time to think economy but not to think society or the other values.

FS: *The pace of change has caught a lot of people by surprise but you've often contended that recent decades are simply the tail end of a far longer cycle. Is that an accurate assessment?*

HB: Yes, absolutely. The seeds of modernity were sown 200 years ago, not in the '90s. I think we have to trace it back that far before we can make any sense of it.

FS: *That's a pretty wide frame of reference. Can we reasonably expect people to grasp that the origins of current trends go back two centuries?*

HB: Well, the fact it hasn't been examined before doesn't make it easy or obvious. Even our reluctance to analyse these issues in depth is typical of how we want everything *now!* Quick analysis, ready solutions. If we are serious about re-directing where we are going, we have to examine how we got here. It's not a lecture or a sermon but it's not a quick-fix either.

FS: *So how can we put modernity into context?*

HB: People who are writing critiques and analysing at the moment are just taking the present as if everything began in the '90s. I don't think you can do that.

If you can identify the significant events of the past, you will immediately see how one step led to the next. It gives us a more serious examination of where we are and what steps may be ahead in the future.

If you think of it, Irish society didn't commemorate the centenary of The Famine because it was still so close to us. People living in the time of the centenary were still connected to those who remembered its aftermath. A hundred years was too close. We commemorated it after 150 years because it was only by moving that bit further on we could remove ourselves from it.

As we know, The Famine had a traumatic effect on the Irish psyche. It left a profound mark on Irish society, going from a population of eight million down to around three million people in a few decades. The experience reverberated long after food was available again in steady supply.

FS: *What was the cultural imprint of The Famine?*

HB: As a nation, it left Ireland spiritually stone dead at the end of the 1870s. The 1880s saw a lot of the revivalist movements — like the GAA, the Gaelic League, the co-operative movement — take off. It also marked the revival of the Catholic Church and so on. We can see now that it almost took something to destroy us before other major influences emerged to reconstruct Irish society. I think there's a parallel there with what is going on at the moment.

FS: *Local or national events play their own role in the process of social change. Apart from the famine, Irish history presents quite a few familiar turning points over the past 200 years.*

HB: In Irish terms, I would see the last century opening with colonialism, then being dominated by clericalism and ending with capitalism. During all this time community action was in many ways the one great buffer to the excesses or dominance of any one influence.

I would argue that we, as a nation, urgently need to construct a national philosophy which will have community at its heart. So the era we're moving into has to be the era of "communitarianism" and I think that's what we have to work out. We need new models of how people can live together.

Economically, we're certainly at our best time — actually in many ways we're at one of the best times in our history. But I see this as the current phase of our evolution. Historical events — like famine, independence, partition, civil war, emigration, joining the EU — all stand out as significant chapters but we have to look deeper. Even if we review the historical path, we can see it doesn't answer a lot of the questions it raises.

FS: *If we need a historical reference to our economic perform-ance, let's take post-famine times as a starting point.*

HB: Okay. Briefly, the revivalist movement became an emerging force towards the end of the 19th century, leading eventually to 1916, independence, partition and civil war. Then we had an economic war, World War and massive emigration through the '50s. And so it was only in the '60s, when every other country in the western world was boom-ing, that Ireland implemented its first economic plan. We got our first taste of economic heaven with the branches of mul-tinationals coming and the government putting programmes in place to attract them here.

That laid the foundation for free education in 1967. We had the communications revolution through television, a world recession in the '80s and by the time we came out of a dip in the '90s we were ready for major investment. The education system laid the foundation for a skilled, English-speaking workforce which attracted large-scale American and European investment. The boom, or what became known as the Celtic Tiger, had arrived.

These are the footnotes of modern Irish history and it's also the standard version of past-to-present. I mean, eco-nomically, it was literally a miracle and very welcome for all that. But it doesn't *explain* anything to us. At least not in so-cial terms.

We've had to get used to the boom. I think we're now learning there's quite a downside to it. There are a lot of young lives being taken, young lives being lost. There's a lot of suffering out there at the moment, a lot of pain surrounding family breakdown.

And so we need to ask ourselves what the connection is between these developments? And what might we learn from what was there before? If we are to consider change, let's take the Church for example. Towards the end of the 19th century, the devotional life of religion was introduced to Ireland from Europe. Looking back, this had serious weaknesses because it undermined the spirituality that came from the heart and soul of people. It shifted religion from a dynamic local community which cared for the poor to people being told what to think, congregations becoming passive and the Church developing as a powerful clerical institution.

That sort of movement had a huge bearing on Irish life and offers some insight into the crisis in which the Catholic Church in Ireland now finds itself.

FS: *The 200-year period you define marked a huge struggle between philosophies — man as a social being or man as an individual. There's probably some crossover between the two but the dominant theory now favours breaking down society into a sum of individuals. What happened to Catholic Church teaching through all of this?*

HB: This idea of society as a collection of individuals was strongly opposed by doctrines of communism and Catholic social teaching. Most significantly however, both schools failed to respond to social change to make their doctrines relevant. There's no mistaking which philosophy won out.

In more recent years, this process accelerated through the Thatcher/Reagan era and we're now at a very critical time when market value is the dominant philosophy.

As participants in the market, we serve our self-interest. However it doesn't serve our self-interest to be nothing but market participants. From my point of view, human beings cannot exist without spiritual nourishment. Neither can we survive freedom without responsibility.

We need to concern ourselves with the wider picture. We're beginning to see that Irish society is paying an unacceptable price for material wealth.

FS: *But as an enthusiastic participant in the global economy is there any way for us to re-draw the rules?*

HB: What I'm saying is we may have reached the pinnacle of the financial world. How much more money has to be played around with?

The global economy is coming apart at the seams because it cannot include, or take account of, some of the most important things in human life. These are to do with relationships, with moral/ethical values, with the environment and our relationship with God.

After 200 years, the Age of Reason is revealing serious limitations. Morality and social values need to be reconstructed. Globalisation, for all its association with free trade or free movement of people/goods/capital, is based on inequality. And the system is designed to maintain that inequality. For example, over half — well, 51 to be exact — of the world's largest 100 economies are made up by global corporations.

Even if you compare individual corporations — the annual spending of companies such as General Motors, Exxon, Ford, IBM, General Electric and/or Mobil Oil matches or exceeds government spending in Canada and the majority of the governments of Europe. Or the Mitsubishi company. It's wealthier than Indonesia, the world's fourth most populous country in the world.

These are all figures and sometimes it's hard to grasp what they really mean, but think about this. The combined sales of the world's top 200 corporations amounts to 28 per cent of the world Gross Domestic Product. The same 200 corporations employ only 18.8 million people, less than 0.3 per cent of the world's population. That's less than half of one per cent!

The critical thing we need to look at is the claim that the common interest is best served by allowing everyone to look out for their own interests. The assumption is that efforts to protect the common interest by collective decision-making will distort the market.

FS: *Why do you highlight the Thatcher-Reagan era in all of this?*

HB: They were key figures in promoting the free market through the 1980s. Their administrations in London and Washington removed almost every restriction on what we call market fundamentalism or market powers. It gave free rein to multinationals around the world, putting money and individualism into the driving seat to the exclusion of social capital and human values in society.

So, on the one hand, we have a sort of independence, almost a freedom to do what we like. But at the same time we have become helpless. Whether it's Rupert Murdoch in the media world or somebody else in the stock market, money which moves freely gets concentrated in fewer hands. When market values become the main shapers of society, a wide range of individual and social values are ignored. The upshot is the beginnings of all sorts of human problems.

FS: *Well, like it or not, we do live in a capitalist system.*

HB: Then it's about time we really started examining that system. Money has become so powerful that the world now revolves around how money is traded. How it is moved from one stock market to another, how it can destroy local economies and what it can do to third world countries. In other words, it's hugely central to national economies.

As we can see, the market is volatile and very vulnerable. It can blow any time — even now, the US is in serious trouble, several Asian stock markets have lost heavily, Russia is in meltdown and Latin America is in crisis. The reality is, financial markets are inherently unstable.

If we're simply going to accept that this is the system as it stands, let's start digging deeper. We should look seriously at the fact that the new millennium began with the largest difference ever recorded between rich and poor countries. Today, the per capita income of the richest 20 countries is almost 40 times higher than that of the 20 poorest countries. In the 1960s, it was less than 20 times higher. So greater economic integration has *widened* the gap.

At the same time, the gap between the rich and poor is also increasing within many countries and regions. From my point of view, the most important part of all this is that market values do take over the shaping of lives. And the social/moral/ethical values — the human values — get very little attention.

Where does that leave us? Major decisions being made primarily on economic grounds. Market values are totally inappropriate in areas like medicine or law and yet there is every indication they are becoming central to these professions. When market values become so powerful that they penetrate into areas of society where they do not properly belong, we begin to have massive social problems.

And so you have family life pushed to the sidelines, more and more of our elderly shunted out of the community and into nursing homes. Or it's well within this kind of thinking that couples might even weigh up a decision between a commodity — such as a new car — or having a baby. These values have wormed their way into social, political and business life in a very dangerous way.

FS: *If the idea of a universal market is so dominant, does anything stand in the way of globalisation?*

HB: I think you need reasonably powerful political entities as a bulwark against the financial markets. Obviously if the political entity in our case is the European Union, you then need to be able to work back from there into fairly strong national governments and even stronger local government.

I have found that the more centralised government becomes, the greater the need to strengthen local government and local power. I see this because one of the great challenges down the road will be the integration of the global with the local.

It may be a cliché, but its no exaggeration to say all politics is local. We might live in a political universe like the EU but we live on the ground in Shannon or County Clare or Dublin, a place with neighbours and community and so on. We need to be able to work from the ground up and above all, we need to rebuild new models of community.

FS: *Is this need specific to Ireland?*

HB: No, but we do have some issues that are particularly relevant to us. I would reiterate that Ireland's economic miracle over the past decade was a most welcome development but there are two areas that require urgent attention. The first relates to public policy and the other is around relationships and the things that give meaning to life. We invested heavily in technological development but seriously neglected areas of the caring services. We continue to demand greater investment in public services and rightly so.

But there is also a great need to invest in the search for community, in the respect for life and relationships. We took the whole world of relationships for granted — parents to children, teachers to students, doctors and nurses to patients. All of these relationships were removed from their natural contexts, where they were seen as intrinsically good, where they were the building blocks of society. Instead, they became the means to a narrow end — progress, the building of the economy.

So, naturally, the relationships themselves became distorted. The things that made these relationships work, the support of society and its institutions, have gradually been eroded or fallen away. We then get shocked when we hear of people taking their own lives. We hear it from all angles — alcohol abuse, drugs, stress-related illnesses, crime.

Right now people are confused. There is an urgent need for ethical and inspirational leadership. There is an obvious need to give children back their innocence, to restore a genuine respect for our elderly, to examine the idea of what we call "work-rich" and "work-poor" families and to wonder what the notion of common good now means in a value-system driven by economic, market and technological factors. We need to rebuild the relationships between people and society for their own sakes, not for some market-driven goal.

FS: *Are you pessimistic about the prospect for future generations?*

HB: I'm not pessimistic because we're in a position to do something about it. What does concern me, however, is the structure of society we're creating with the Information Age. From the mass media we get instant and constant news about the world situation, about wars, oppression, hunger, the spread of AIDS and inequalities of all sorts.

The feedback we get from young people is they don't know what to do with all this information. This is key. They feel helpless and guilty. The world appears to be chaotic if you listen to that every day — massive wealth on one hand and appalling deprivation on the other.

Science and technology are producing incredible techniques for knowing and doing but the impact of the mass media is having the opposite effect. Instead of bringing enlightenment, many young people find the Information Age frightening and confusing. It breeds a type of helplessness — the sort Peter Abbott referred to — that discourages people from doing anything about it.

FS: *Are we underestimating the resilience of younger generations? Or maybe expecting too much?*

HB: I don't think so, because I see major changes going on. When Ireland experienced the economic, education and communications revolution in the 1960s, young people dreamed dreams. The student revolutions of that period were searching for an alternative society, alternative ways of living and alternative communities. They felt they could do something about it. They could throw away the old and take the risk of building the new. There was great excitement about it. We need to rekindle that spark.

Without it, we'll get a different picture from young people all over the country. They feel insecure, rootless or unclear as to what they want. They feel helpless and guilty in the face of pain or problems. Many feel apathetic and fall into a world of depression, seeking compensation in gangs, hard rock, drugs and superficial sex. They are desperately seeking to fill the emptiness of their lives.

Or else they choose to throw themselves into the established ways, working hard at school, getting a job and trying to forget all the rest in their search for security on solid ground.

Young people are in desperate need of identity. They are looking for a community in which they can re-find their deeper selves and experience values that give a certain structure to their lives. So there's a lot of confusion.

FS: *If we accept that the development of capitalism went hand-in-hand with the rise of individualism, does the global success of capitalism mean you can't have one without the other?*

HB: Well, that's how people will see it, especially now that the traditional institutions have ceased to lead. All this prosperity is so welcome to us because it's in such contrast to the poverty we've had for so long in this country. It's the same all over the world.

Prosperity is always going to be attractive. I think the linkage of both schools was — or is — inevitable to the point of individualism and self-interest being taken too far, to the point of us not being able to live with one another.

The sequence of debate has to be, firstly, identifying the issues and then working out practical approaches to restore the balance. That's going to take serious investment.

Let me give you a practical example. Céifin is carrying out a major study on the family in Ireland. We appreciate that after a series of meetings, the Department of Social, Community and Family Affairs supported us with funding. On the day I went up to discuss the project in Dublin a news bulletin on the radio announced that the Tánaiste was investing another half a billion euro in research for science and technology. That half a billion is probably well justified, but so too is research funding for the study of the family. The thing is, if the family collapses, there'll be no need for technology.

The point is, we continue to invest in the technological world and the scientific world and so on. Not only have we forgotten the other things but we haven't invested in trying to discover a type of social organisation to help restore the balance, one which doesn't promote "self" but which will make us aware of others.

And that has to be worked at. It'll have to start right at the very beginning.

FS: *Ideally, you'd like to open up the debate?*

HB: Yes, because people are lapsing into whatever is on offer — insecurity with all the anguish that implies; or of false security through power, work, material values, sex, drugs. Let's get beyond this current set of options.

What we're interested in is the broader alternative. Let's get back to a community where people can grow with openness and sharing. From what I see and hear, I believe young people are hugely interested in this.

The danger for individuals, groups and nations is to close themselves off to an idea like this. If we're not open to this type of communitarianism, it will leave a vacuum which will be filled by fundamentalism or fanaticism. I don't think that leaders of church and state really appreciate the urgent need for changes for the young and their world.

FS: *It seems that themes and concerns raised by the Céifin conferences have struck a chord with people across the entire spectrum of society. What's particularly surprising is that a number of business leaders, who have succeeded in this competitive climate, are also subscribing to the debate. If they have shown themselves capable of doing well in the present marketplace, why should they want to get involved in this?*

HB: Firstly, many have said to me they have become involved in this because they have children themselves. They are parents. When I asked the assistant chief executive of a very big corporation why he was interested he said he had children himself and he wasn't comfortable with the kind of Ireland they're growing up in.

The second reason they are coming in is because there's an awareness beginning to dawn on corporate leaders in Ireland that a corporation or a business cannot flourish in an environment that disregards the family and community. Even from a purely subjective viewpoint, the large-scale business or corporation will have to be more involved or they won't get the workforce they want.

Success has become so important in the kind of world we live in. Obviously, there are a lot of successful people who work their business honestly and justly and fairly. It can be done and we want to get that across.

As for the conferences, the funny thing is I admit I wasn't particularly enthusiastic about them in the first place. I didn't know what would sort of interest they would generate and I certainly didn't want them to end up as talk-shops.

I have to say I was bowled over by how the conferences have been received. From the very first one in Ennis, it was obvious enough that we had tapped into something big. Over and over we could see how Ireland's economic progress had left social, spiritual and personal life behind. People want to address these issues and they want to come on board.

FS: *This is beginning to sound like a Japanese-style set-up where the corporation becomes a sort of enclosed universe for everybody associated with it.*

HB: The Japanese model is well worth exploring, although it is not as successful now as it was in the past. Japanese companies seem to take a very broad view of their role in society, which is something I would regard as a positive.

For example, the company motto at Mitsui Corporation is Ten-Chi-Jin (Heaven-Earth-Human Beings). Mitsui describes its purpose in the following order: (1) to contribute to Japanese society, to serve the greater glory of Japan; (2) to realise profit for the company so as to promote the welfare and happiness of its employees; and (3) to foster and strengthen the spirit for the future as set forth in the company motto. The satisfaction of shareholders is only a means to those ends.

FS: *It sounds good but Japan is not the economic force it was twenty years ago.*

HB: Their priority was to rebuild Japan. That remains the primary motivation to this day, although Japan hardly needs to be "rebuilt" at this stage.

Companies are not motivated by profit as such — in Japan there is no public–private partnership as we know it. Most businesses are effectively franchises of the state and their primary motivation is to further the national cause. In the post-war years it was this drive to rebuild that turned Japan into the biggest manufacturer in the world. Internationally, it also became the second biggest economy in the world.

Seeing as Japan is still working to its post-war goal, it is now effectively over-producing goods for the market. The Japanese economy needs to change from being producer-led to people-led but their reluctance to do that is a major problem.

FS: *If the Japanese model is losing ground, is there anything useful Ireland can draw from it?*

HB: Maybe the lesson is that we need more business organisations and institutions whose objectives and goals are more in line with the common good.

Studies clearly indicate that people are the first to go when there's a hiccup in business — even in companies that claim in their mission statements to put people first. These kinds of contradictions are not going to be accepted by the community any more. The kind of things that are beginning to happen — and a number of interested companies are involved with us — is that each company should revisit its mission statement and objectives every quarter, just as they review their profit and loss position. In fact this was something Bewley's Cafés Ltd. in Dublin did every quarter, a type of social audit that originated from their Quaker principles.

I don't think it's acceptable that a corporation should exist in isolation from its surroundings. The whole business world has to start adapting itself more and more to the rest of the community and ultimately, I could see it becoming law for corporations to have social audits in the same way they have financial audits.

FS: *So you are suggesting that, apart from personal concerns about the social cost of the boom, it serves commercial interests to get involved in a humanist debate. More likely, a happier workforce will be more productive?*

HB: If employers don't look after people, their profits are going to suffer, whether through absenteeism or productivity or whatever. There's an obvious need for the business world to become as concerned about how healthy the community is.

Even if the motivation for doing so is commercially driven, these wider responsibilities have to be taken very seriously.

Part Two

Confronting History

FS: *When you speak of the failure of institutions, what institutions are you referring to?*

HB: The family and community are the basic building blocks of society. They are the systems that held Irish society together for generations. The family was the school of enterprise and education, of formation and nurturing. Traditionally, the powerful relationship between family and community has been an outstanding feature of Irish life.

Next to the family, the most influential social unit has been groupings of families, sharing social and economic life, addressing itself to the task of survival. This takes many forms such as the cluster of neighbourhoods, the townlands, the village. In an institutional sense, the wider community was shaped by religion (Church), sport (GAA), and education (school).

FS: *Excluding the GAA — and Clare hurling! — how have these institutions fared in times of prosperity?*

HB: They are less relevant. They were strong in a stable environment but need to reform in a significant way in order to cope with modernisation.

FS: *But these institutions had grown strong over the past 200 years. What sent them into decline?*

HB: I believe they became complacent and didn't take on board how much society was changing.

In poorer times, the real definition of community was not just family but groupings of families and neighbours that helped one another socially and economically. More recently, there has been a general move away from community towards this emphasis on self. That has brought about a serious change in our definition of things.

Recently, a good friend of mine — a hurling man still in his forties — told me that when he was growing up he knew exactly what club he belonged to, *where* he belonged. He says that his young son doesn't have any of that. The man used to know his neighbours but his son doesn't know them at all. In other words, an important part of identity has been broken.

FS: *Is this another argument in favour of bad-but-happy old days?*

HB: Not at all, but I think we threw out some things we could have tried to hold onto. This trend towards individualism had a disastrous effect on our sense of community. If you consider that half the population of Ireland now live in areas with common addresses but without any semblance of neighbour knowing neighbour, you have to question what sort of society is emerging.

Sometimes I wonder about the planning that brought that about. We don't know how people feel about it because nobody ever asked them. That's one of the areas of research I feel we need to get involved in.

I'm not saying that people shouldn't have privacy. Neither am I assuming that everybody is unhappy with the way it is — maybe the current model is exactly what some people want, without interference from neighbours — but I think these questions have to be researched and examined.

FS: *It is an area light on empirical study but might we draw anything from what we do know?*

HB: I'm not sure. Geographic boundaries are not as relevant as before when we talk about community. Maybe the older sense of the term may not be possible any more. But the basic thing is that people do need people. That's a simple truth but still it gets overlooked.

Of recent social developments, I think it's quite interesting that communities are now more likely to be found in workplaces than where you live. That's a big change. Maybe that's more of an urban phenomenon but it's one worth examining.

The most important thing is to acknowledge that individualism has taken over, yet — and this is what we need to stress — *community is needed.* A new model of community is what we're talking about. That's what we're working towards with Céifin, building up networks around the country and bringing together people from different sectors. If we don't involve a cross-section of society, it's not going to work.

FS: *These are uncomfortable times for official institutions. Would you feel these difficulties were inevitable?*

HB: Where difficulties arise because of a failure to adapt, I would have to say that yes, they were inevitable. On the plus side, I think that lessons have been learned. Previously dominant institutions are beginning to realise that they must adapt to stay relevant.

FS: *In looking at the present situation, why do you trace it back to the industrial revolution?*

HB: I refer back to that period because societal progress since then lived up to most expectations — even surpassed them in the economic arena — but failed to deliver on social thinking and political development.

The seeds of modernity were sown at the end of the nineteenth century. The combination of scientific discoveries and philosophical developments paved the way for the primacy of reason and the power of man. That remains the dominant thinking today.

The long-term impact of the industrial revolution was that production levels and living standards rose to heights unimaginable in any previous age. Despite these impressive achievements, the social evolution that accompanied them has never been critically analysed or examined.

FS: *Where does the Catholic Church fit into this?*

HB: It might come as a surprise to many that the Catholic Church's response to this revolution was both immediate and very powerful, with the first Social Encyclical of Pope Leo XIII in 1891. This was followed by a number of extremely important documents and has continued to the present day within the Church.

These documents made such an impact that a United Nations General Secretary once stated that the most powerful social message in the world is that of the Catholic Church. I don't think anybody can doubt this.

FS: *That probably would surprise people. What sort of influence has the social gospel brought to bear?*

HB: I believe these teachings have been a vital counterbalance to the world of technology. They very firmly underline the dignity of every human being and the rights of individuals and communities.

They also provide clear principles, such as the Principle of Subsidiarity, which supports constructing social organisations with a clear outline of the values that underpin society. This Principle also holds that no higher organisation should undermine that of lower organisations. I think what we have here is a clear guideline for the remodelling of society with an emphasis on the local community.

There are of course very significant Church voices and witnesses to the rights of the under-privileged. It must also be said that, for many years in Ireland, particularly in the '50s, '60s and '70s, the Irish Church produced important documents such as *The Work of Justice*. However, it was harder to apply these directives as Irish society became part of and influenced by the wider western world.

FS: *With so much theological work being done behind the scenes, why did the Catholic Church lose so heavily on the ground?*

HB: I think the main thrust of the social gospel seems to have taken a back seat. Indeed, the failure of the Catholic Church to provide a sufficiently robust body of social doctrine to challenge the power of centralised bureaucracy remains one of the great lost opportunities of Irish intellectual endeavour.

Instead, the Church has been very preoccupied with internal problems and has tended to lose its focus on societal problems. Yet the fact is that the message of Jesus Christ was never more relevant than today.

I just think that instead of being so concerned with internal matters like a shortage of priests, the Church has to be concerned with trying to understand the reality of people's lives.

The Vatican II document *The Church in the Modern World* urged the Church at every level to engage with the world. So the Church has to take its own message seriously and reach out to the realities of life for people. The Irish Church has been too preoccupied with maintenance. The call today is for mission.

FS: *What was so significant about that Vatican II directive?*

HB: The intention of Vatican II was to renew the Church in the context of a world shaped more and more by market values. It simply called on the Church to read the signs of the times — the reality of people's lives — and interpret them in the light of the Gospel. It also recognised the need to proclaim the Gospel message in a language that people could understand.

This was a major shift from proclaiming doctrines from "on high", a practice which compartmentalised religion and distanced it from the lived experience.

Martin Kennedy, a layman involved in pastoral ministry in Offaly, put it this way in an article in *Intercom*,

> "Often we didn't seem to notice that what we had to offer — by virtue of the way we were offering it — was experienced by many good people as bad news."

If we had taken the message of Vatican II seriously, the Church's mission would have started with "where people are" in the world. From there we could address what really matters to people and search for values, presenting a theology in a language that makes sense in responding to those needs.

FS: *Why can't that start now?*

HB: Of course it can — and there are very positive signs that it already has. But we must be convinced that we have to take our own message seriously. We have to realise that for many, religion has been pushed to the margins of everyday life.

FS: *Where is the room for manoeuvre?*

HB: We have to ask ourselves: what must we do in order to be faithful to Tradition? For example, the Catholic Church has been very much a sacramental Church. Some of these sacraments have lost their meaning. Some have simply become social occasions.

Christianity is challenged by new questions that are totally different to those of even the first half of the twentieth century in Ireland. Loyalty to the Church Christ founded demands developing structures and ministries which best serve the communication of the Good News in the context of the culture of our time. That's where we have to start looking.

FS: *It's not too late?*

HB: No — indeed we need to debate these issues now whilst we still have an extraordinarily high practice rate. We also need to get to it while we still have such a large number of people looking to the Christian ethos for meaning in their lives.

There are of course many other problems the Church has to contend with, such as secularisation and a general crisis regarding the credibility of the Christian faith. But none of these should deter the Church of our time from approaching all of these in an open, honest and responsible way.

FS: *How exactly did the Church get bogged down as an institution?*

HB: Between 1850 and 1950, the number of priests in Ireland grew six-fold while the Church here borrowed more and more from the continental model of devotional life. The energy went into Church building.

Powerful movements towards clericalisation and devotional life shifted the world of spirituality away from the people's everyday world. It gave the Church greater control over people's lives and created a stable environment which demanded obedience from the people. In our new understanding of "Church" this new division between "clerics" and "laity" reduced the laity to a very passive role.

I think it's widely recognised at this stage that we have to move in the opposite direction. We need to involve people in the Church, to activate a faith that has become passive.

FS: *Charges of paedophilia against individual priests have led to detailed allegations of a cover-up by the Catholic Church to protect its own. What sort of damage was wrought by recent scandals?*

HB: This has been a horrific experience for us all. Our hearts go out to those who have been abused, to those in authority who have to cope with it and indeed the abusers. I think we have all been hurt and damaged — both by what the victims have had to suffer and by the way Church leaders handled the situation. There's been a massive toll and there's no doubt the constant stream of scandals has really sapped the morale of many priests.

However, out of every crisis — cruel and all as the crisis might be — comes a serious wake-up call and indeed, opportunity. We must have the courage to grasp the opportunity that now presents itself. We must remember that fear is one of the great obstacles to moving forward. We can't succumb to it — we can't afford to.

FS: *Given public reaction to date, lying low would be understandable.*

HB: We can't deny the extent of hurt and damage but what are we going to do — hide away? The best leaders in any walk of life are those who have a great sense of confidence in the future of what they are about. Risk is part of it. It would be ironic if Church people today were paralysed by fear when we consider that the opposite of fear is faith.

Martin Kennedy wrote elsewhere in *Intercom* that the scandals shook the Church out of "a deep-rooted institutional arrogance". He said we could only be glad for some good coming out of evil. I fully agree — and he definitely hit on something when he added:

> "But I do regret what has often replaced our arrogance — silence, keeping our heads down. While this is understandable it is not what we are here for."

FS: *Given the institutional bearing of the Church, was this a fall from grace waiting to happen?*

HB: Well it didn't have to happen but once it did, it was very important for us to deal openly and honestly with it. Priests live between a layer of bishops and the laity. It puts us in the centre of a hierarchical organisation but while we want to be loyal to the bishops and the Pope in Rome, the people represent our Church. And it's the people that we serve. They are the Church.

The scandals hastened what was coming but they were not the sole cause of a major shift in the Church's influence on society. I don't want to understate the suffering that people experienced but we should realise the damage caused by how these scandals were handled. Protecting the institution was ingrained in clerical leaders for some time and this mentality was seriously exposed when confronted with this challenge.

FS: *If this was fifty years ago, the Church would have been capable of burying those scandals.*

HB: Yes, because as Garret Fitzgerald recently pointed out, Irish society and Irish political life was deferential towards the Church and Church authority, thus giving it extraordinary control over people's lives. It was only when a Church became one influence among many others that accountability became a real issue.

FS: *Which brings us to the present . . .*

HB: The social and cultural change Ireland is now experiencing is deep and pervasive. The forces driving this change are at work throughout the western world, affecting different countries differently but presenting many common features. There is no escaping this new culture, no safe haven. The forces driving it and shaping it are getting stronger.

Clearly, in many respects this new culture is at odds with the Gospel. Its inspirations are not rooted in the Christian tradition. Its values, models and thinking are often opposed to it. In short, it is a non-Christian culture but even so, there are many positive elements in it.

People are searching for meaning. I'm utterly convinced institutions need to face up to this as a matter of urgency. There is certainly a very radical choice now facing the Irish Church. The challenge is obvious but it is vital that it doesn't wait until it is too late.

FS: *But the Catholic Church can't change the world on its own — especially in its present working condition.*

HB: That's absolutely true but the Church can play a major role in the rehabilitation of core values within society. The Church does not have a copyright on values. They are incorporated in international documents, in the constitutions of Governments and in the mission statements of corporations.

But values, morals and ethics are intrinsic to the nature of organised religion. Most people have a set of core values but the speed and excesses of modern life are such as to leave little time to identify what they are and apply them to real life. Christian values are intrinsic to the nature of the Church. It could have a great role in reawakening individuals and organisations to revisit their core values.

FS: *You contend that change can begin at local level. Is this an opportunity to start such a process?*

HB: It certainly is. In fact, many dioceses in Ireland are now engaging in this search. Basically, they are posing the question: what does the Church stand for? This is a different emphasis from what it is against.

In our own diocese we are now involved in a fairly major planning exercise. We began by getting involved in a listening survey. We identified twenty focus groups — from students to Travellers to teachers to priests — in an effort to listen to their stories and their concerns.

We then moved on to identify what the "Good News" has to say to that reality.

I believe that this is a hugely hopeful sign. There is a very clear message emerging that tells us religious faith demands spiritual practice. There is an urgent need to identify what this actually consists of. In practice it is a call for a radical re-orientation away from our habitual preoccupation with self, towards concern for the wider community.

In all of this, there is a call for people within the Christian community to let go of positions which are holding us back and to begin journeying together, searching, listening, learning, opening dialogue and challenging.

FS: *It sounds almost revolutionary.*

HB: It does in a way but it shouldn't! Over the last forty years, the Church has invested massive money in church buildings. There is now an urgent need to invest in people, in ministries and in new ways of doing things.

In a sense, the last few years have been a period of purification leading now to serious efforts to bring the Church into a new era.

There are obviously major problems regarding credibility, the issue of clerical power and indeed with coping with change. But the opportunity is there to respond to people's need for meaning.

FS: *If the Church does not build places of worship, where should the effort go?*

HB: When Jesus met the Samaritan woman, he told her that the place of worship is not nearly as important as her attitude towards worship. There is a clear message in this for us today.

For the last number of years, we have been investing heavily in the material, externals of life. But there are clear indications that there's a need for spiritual nourishment. The question for the Church is: how is it going to respond to that need? That's a major question. That immediately brings into question the over-reliance the Church had on external devotions at the expense of inner spirituality.

The area of justice — who speaks for the poor? What voice have they got? I would say that the Church of the future has to be a Church of the poor and broken, spiritually and materially. Maybe for too long we have been forgetting that Christ came to save sinners.

The Christ I know from the Gospels is the one who walked the journeys of life with people. He didn't lecture the two young lads on the road to Emmaus. He didn't tell them about "Church". He asked, "What's your story?" He first befriended them. He walked the road with confused people, poor people and I think we have to do that today. All of us.

FS: *You and I first met to discuss the Kilanena-Flagmount community in East Clare, the first parish in Ireland to function without a parish priest. Considering the dramatic fall-off in vocations and the ageing profile of the Catholic clergy, it's surprising that it* *hadn't happened before. You weren't surprised by developments at Kilanena and argued it should have happened sooner for different reasons. Can you elaborate on your support for what's now known as "the priestless parish"?*

HB: A few years ago, diocesan changes in Killaloe diocese left the parish of Kilanena/Flagmount without a priest in residence. It also left its parishioners in a state of shock. For the first time in history, the local people were left wondering who would look after their pastoral needs and tend to their spiritual lives.

With every justification, they questioned how their local church and their religious life would endure. Its administration had always been the responsibility of their local priest. Hurt and confused, the people were also frightened by this development. They were totally ill-equipped to deal with this situation. Who would say their anniversary masses? Bury their dead? Marry their sons and daughters and celebrate the christening of their children? Would they have to "borrow" a priest from another parish to conduct various services? With nobody specifically appointed to tend to their spiritual needs they wondered what priest would get to know them as individuals and care for them as a people?

The people needed to voice their fears. This was done at public meetings. The Bishop, Willie Walsh, attended these meetings. He listened to the people. Eventually, it was agreed that the Church and the people would work in partnership, supporting one another in identifying a new way forward and redefining the role of community within the Church.

It was agreed that a priest would be available for essential church services and that the diocese would provide the necessary help and guidance to establish a new structure and new ways of tackling the individual needs of the community.

So, that parish embarked on a new chapter in its history, developing a way forward in its relationship with the Diocese. With support and training, the people began to take responsibility for the management of their own parish and its affairs.

FS: *In what way was Kilanena handled badly?*

HB: The situation arose out of necessity and not from any grand plan. The people were totally unprepared. They wondered why they were singled out as the only parish in the country and of course they were hurt.

But they did rise to the challenge and there was a lot to be learned from it.

The question of people identifying their own pastoral needs and working in partnership to address those needs was crucial. The fact that day-to-day management of the parish — including finances — became the responsibility of the people had the two-fold effect of people participation and releasing a priest to administer to the pastoral needs of the parish.

However, if this model is to become the pattern around the country, obviously there's a lot of work to do regarding the transition. It also highlights the need for priests to work in teams rather than an individual priest being confined to a single parish. And of course the whole question of the numbers of Masses and churches has to be addressed.

FS: *The decline in vocations to the priesthood in Ireland is quite spectacular — from 1980 to 1996, the number of diocesan clergy fell from 3,998 to 3,616. Surely the shortage of priests presents a major predicament for the Church in future years?*

HB: In a sense it does. However, if we are serious about genuine participation and allowing the people to become the real force within the Church then we now have very clear reasons for moving in this direction.

It means of course that the role of the priest needs to be examined. It is important that both partners — people and priests — are open to change and that both are comfortable with the re-evaluation of traditional roles. Adhering to the "old way" will only provide obstacles to the evolution of a new relationship between the Church and its followers.

As we begin this journey at the start of a new millennium we are only returning to what was a genuine religion of the people, *Pobal Dé*, which existed at the beginning of the nineteenth century. At that time, the Catholic Church in Ireland had about 400 priests, mostly Franciscans and Dominicans. It was a folk Church, institutionally weak, with relatively low Mass attendance.

The people were known as *Pobal Dé*, the People of God. The Church was the house of God. Theirs was a deep-rooted spirituality grounded in everyday life.

FS: *Do you see any connection between then and now?*

HB: Yes, I do. I think we could learn a lot from those practices if we want to work towards a spiritual revival in the Ireland of today.

I think it's significant that at the height of *Pobal Dé* Irish people were experiencing extreme poverty, a serious "brokenness" in the survival of daily life. Now that we're in a period of prosperity, we tend to get distracted from our spiritual lives by staying in the comfort zone. We become consumers to help us ignore the reality of our lives.

We forget that Christianity was founded on the hill of Calvary — in other words, Christianity was born out of "brokenness". Touching into spiritual poverty must be the way forward for Christian renewal.

FS: *Do we need priests at all?*

HB: Priests still hold pivotal positions within the Church. They are central to the whole concept of a Christian community but our image of the priest has changed since Vatican II. Up to the early '60s, the priest tended to be depicted as something of an angel, as one who "lived in the midst of the world with no desire for its pleasures".

After the Vatican Council, a prayer inspired by Karl Rahner depicted the priest as one who remains human and Christian. Someone who needs the prayers and support of the people. In other words, the priest was to become one who would fulfil his ministry through being *with* the people rather than "doing things" for them.

FS: *Do you feel the priest is taken for granted — both within the Church and by the people?*

HB: Yes, I do. What's more, I think it's very evident that this attitude needs to challenged. The fact is that priesthood is no longer the social reality it once was. Ministerial roles are less clear than before and for these and other reasons, it's time that the man at the "coalface" is not taken for granted anymore. That said, I believe the humanity of people as priests is finally gaining recognition.

FS: *Has the priest's role changed so significantly?*

HB: Most definitely. Indeed there is some confusion among priests — and among people generally — as to the essential nature of the priesthood. Every priest is being left to work out his own answer to this question.

It doesn't help that, even within the Church, the priest's mission has become blurred. Vatican II underlined the authority of Bishop *and* defined the Church as the one people of God. This has led to widespread uncertainty as to the priest's role.

Meanwhile on the ground the priest is called on to implement new ministries or become involved in collaborative ministry with little, if any, training. Before Vatican II, the priest was defined by his sacramental duties and powers, mainly through the celebration of the Eucharist. To some extent, those very sacraments have become social occasions, leading to even further diminution of his role.

The priest on the ground has also borne the brunt of public anxiety following recent Church scandals. At a pastoral level, he has to cope with a lot of difficult situations without any back-up — for instance, there are few priests who haven't had to deal with suicide cases and the effect this has on families.

There is a feeling among clergy that the priest's role has become more complex, yet more ambiguous and more isolated. A lot of support which existed in the past no longer exists and I believe there is a clear need for the Church to take far more care of its clergy in modern Ireland.

FS: *That certainly puts the decline in vocations into perspective. However, if the role of priests can be redefined, do the numbers really matter?*

HB: The role of priests has to change with the times. Equally, the spirituality of the people, *Pobal Dé*, needs to be revived so that the actual number of priests is even less of an issue. The reality is, there is still a strong religious sensibility in Ireland but the Church is not connecting with it. That is the challenge facing us.

Historically, there were only 400 priests in Ireland in 1800 but by the 1860s the Catholic Church was completely transformed. About 2,000 churches were built in 60 years and the number of vocations increased accordingly. A century later, with the general population in serious decline, there were six times more priests in Ireland!

Clericalism took over. The Church had so many full-time officials — priests, nuns, brothers — that they ran everything. Religious practices were introduced at the expense of personal spirituality.

I do feel the Church made a huge contribution to many aspects of life in Ireland during that period. The point now is that times have changed and the challenge now is to respond to that change.

FS: *Would you like to see a return to* Pobal Dé?

HB: It isn't a question of "liking" a return to *Pobal Dé*. For all kinds of reasons, it is necessary to take this whole concept of Church very seriously.

The next few years will see a huge drop in the number of priests ministering in Ireland while the general population will increase considerably. In our diocese, we will see each priest ministering on average to four times as many people as in the 1970s.

Furthermore, the information we are gathering from a range of focus groups indicate two very strong patterns. One is very positive and one very negative.

On the one hand, it's clear there is still a real openness to faith and religious values among all ages. There is a desire for a Church that can connect with and be relevant to the lives of people. On the other hand, it is equally clear that the Church is not connecting well with people, particularly the younger generations. There is a sense of the Church becoming less and less relevant.

It is obvious from all of this that the way parishes are organised will have to change radically. The massive change in the ratio of priests to people makes that inevitable. It is also obvious that fresh approaches to ministry are needed if we are to connect with that openness to spirituality among younger age groups. All this poses huge questions about how best the Church should proceed from here. It will certainly involve training, organisational change, people taking ownership of their Church.

FS: *Introducing new systems sounds easier in theory than in practice. The Catholic Church is essentially a conservative movement and as we saw in Kilanena-Flagmount, radical change is not always so welcome.*

HB: This is absolutely true. It is always difficult to get from analysis to application. However, the first steps must be taken and then at least it is a question of moving in the right direction.

Society is at a critical stage. There are major social, moral, ethical issues to be addressed. In that context, it is vital that the Church identifies how Christianity can dialogue with the world to work out how the great message of Christianity can permeate people's lives. It goes back to our earlier discussion of a social gospel.

The Kilanena experience only happened because there was a shortage of priests. However, the one clear message for me out of this is the vital importance in searching for the positive and for solutions.

Every so often, civilisation seems to work itself into a corner from which further progress seems virtually impossible. What happened in Kilanena looked very ominous at first but having worked through it with the people, I believe we'll have a stronger Church at the end of it.

If new ideas are to have a chance the old systems must be so severely shaken that they lose their complacency. I believe we're going through that process at this time.

FS: *People power is always a persuasive catch-cry but this idea of regeneration seems to appeal to you as a means of institutions starting over.*

HB: There will always be a need for institutions but this is a major wake-up call. We have to look forward. All institutions need to take a serious look at themselves to adapt to the reality of people's everyday lives.

FS: *Why should other institutions find themselves in the same boat?*

HB: For a start, they've been found out. The people who broke trust for the most part were people who assumed power. From now on, respect will have to be earned. Up to now, people were compliant. Now they're not and they won't be any more. They're going to question a lot of what goes on.

A lot of the judicial tribunals and examinations that are going on at the moment are basically a society confronting its history. It's good for us as a society to do that. Hopefully there will be a change of direction because this goes to the very heart of key institutions like Church and State. This will be absolutely key in building up a new communitarian society.

If people are to live together and share this planet, it's fundamental that they trust one another. It's terribly important that the cleansing that's going on at the moment leads to something positive, a better way of doing things.

This form of self-examination is probably necessary to bring us forward. Whether we progress or not is another thing but ordinary people cannot be taken for granted like that any more.

FS: *People might be more wary of authority than before but it seems a little optimistic to imagine institutions suddenly adopting transparent power structures. Where can real change happen?*

HB: The present confrontation with history is hugely significant. Some things that were part of our culture in the past will no longer be acceptable. How individuals respond to change is one side of the story. The other will be the response of institutions and organisations.

We have come through a period of disillusionment with almost all large organisations. Words that come to mind are betrayal, inflexibility, "out of touch", irrelevance. If the institutions that held society together cannot be trusted, people become cynical and eventually experience a crisis in values.

FS: *Do you see any evidence of an ethical new world?*

HB: I certainly see the need for one. When a culture undergoes major change, some of the old norms clearly become redundant. But, what can easily happen is that values which are very important can be discarded as well as those that are regarded as out of date.

FS: *Do values change?*

HB: Yes, all the time. Indeed one of the most critical problems facing our society is what values or ideals are being passed on to young people. Most people agree this is a key issue but in our present culture we find it almost impossible to work this out in a practical way.

In the past in Ireland, the Catholic Church played an enormous part in defining values. Other influences have come into play and the dominant ethos is now "mé féinism". Individual freedom is now considered the most important value in Western society.

The Céifin approach is about identifying our personal values and drawing from the values we espouse within our various organisations. In this way, we believe that society must arrive at a set of shared and articulated values that creates a link between our basic attitudes and our behaviour.

The fact is, words like ethics, morality, values are almost becoming discredited. They are rarely discussed in a serious way. Governments and big organisations have been criticised for a lack of vision and direction but this only reflects a failure on the part of people generally agreeing a set of values that would form the basis of such a vision.

Of course, individual freedom is an important value but it must include people living up to personal responsibility — whether in the family, local community or wider society. This applies in other areas too.

FS: *When we look at abuses of power in the political arena, is there really a sense of betrayal out there? Or is it viewed — even accepted — as insiders simply playing the system?*

HB: Trust has been broken. It's as simple as that. People who held — and still hold — positions of power betrayed the confidence people placed in them. The damage has gone deep and as we've seen in politics, business, religion, people have reacted with cynicism and/or apathy. It will take a long time to undo that damage.

FS: *Cynicism and apathy are nothing new in times of plenty. After all, if it ain't broke, why fix it?*

HB: Betrayal is one of two themes that arose most forcibly when we started looking at changes in society — the other was globalisation. The key to betrayal is that a younger generation was betrayed by an older generation.

When we were growing up we bowed the knee to figures like the bank manager, the clergyman, the politician and so on. Each of them represented these institutions — "pillars of society" as they say — and it was from public confidence in the system that they drew their authority.

But there has been a serious breach of trust. I would say that the leadership of the future has to be one that restores trust. And in practice that means words alone carry no weight any more. People believe you and trust you only for what you do and not what you say.

FS: *Can this happen quickly — if it happens at all?*

HB: That's a question we've asked ourselves many times. Obviously this is something that we want to promote as part of values-led change, but it's already quite clear it won't happen overnight.

I often think of Eric Hoffer's maxim: "In times of change, learners inherit the earth while the learned find themselves beautifully equipped to deal with a world that no longer exists."

The need for reform is now well-established and we must begin with the listening process.

FS: *Can you give us a typical example?*

HB: I could give many examples but what surprises me is that *in spite of all that has happened* institutions continue to distrust people and local communities. It's most obvious when you find obstacles being put in the way of local communities by "institution people".

I'd see it as a question of trust. I've come across it myself — for example, pursuing a project of major significance for a rural community in County Clare, we had a specific proposal for government. It led to dealing with a particular government body over the past three years. To our great satisfaction, we were initially told by the relevant officials that our project was innovative, that it was badly needed on the ground and that it would be supported by that particular government body.

And then we waited and waited. Two and a half years have passed and still we are waiting. Numerous attempts to get information on the status of our project have failed. We have been given the run around without explanation and frequently without the courtesy of a response to our letters and calls.

To me, it says that this government body does not believe local people can deliver this project but it is not prepared to state this view. Instead, the officials have virtually cut off communication and from afar they promise us decisions that never come. This has been a sobering lesson in trust, or more precisely the lack of trust, that can exist between the state and the local community.

With power comes the responsibility to build trust. The State, the EU and their institutions must use their immense power to reach across to local communities, not through mission statements but through action. Only in this way will trust be reciprocated by local communities.

A second personal experience relates to a community hospital of which I am chairman. In our efforts to secure public funding for our services, to which the same public body has told us that we are entitled, we have had to attend thirteen meetings with an average of four public servants per meeting. What should be a relatively straightforward task has been turned into a test of endurance. Why should it be so? What is it that we are so afraid of in each other?

Local communities fully accept that they must be responsible with the management of public funds but trust must be more forthcoming from the institutions of the State.

The scandals of the past did not emanate from local communities but from those who held power over them, in various forms. Trust was not broken by ordinary communities and people but by the "power-full". Those who hold power have a solemn responsibility to build trust with others and to do this at an individual level as well as through their collective force.

FS: *Is officialdom that far removed from local initiative?*

HB: Don't get me wrong. The vast majority of public servants in Ireland are seriously dedicated people. However, the extent of such centralised administrative services for such a small population seems to be totally out of proportion to what is required.

In the absence of a shared value system, of people taking responsibility for themselves, bureaucracies grow, new laws proliferate and eventually we come to believe that society can only survive through more of the same.

That's not what we need. It's quite clear to me that we could not only survive but prosper by returning to a communitarian movement.

FS: *What about the private sector?*

HB: The private sector is of course a key player. Most people within that sector are risk-takers, who generate wealth and provide jobs for so many others. But in a society without a shared value system, they must come to appreciate their social responsibilities.

Financial services are particularly vital within any society. Banks are powerful institutions but the only reason they are powerful is that they control people's money. I would love to see us apply the philosophy of "the people's bank" — the German banking system at the end of the nineteenth century. That system was based on the idea that money deposited in an area was reinvested in that area.

I see huge opportunities for restructuring finance around this concept. Take the west of Ireland, which has always been regarded as the underdeveloped part of the country. Financial institutions have constantly siphoned money *away* from there to build office blocks in London and elsewhere. Or another example — in 1994, Irish Pension funds had £500 million of Irish money invested abroad.

I fully realise that we are part of a wider world but it is important we strike a balance between the needs of the local and those of the global. In working ourselves into a communitarian, era it is vital we tackle these types of issues.

FS: *Is it possible that we are demonising every institution and making angels out of every local initiative?*

HB: Yes, it is possible. Without a shared value system, without basic trust, we can come to see almost everyone and everything in productive terms and in terms of personal gain.

I have always believed that once a society begins to abuse its land it will then come to abuse its natural environment, its animals and eventually its people. When we come to see a tree purely in terms of how much timber it can produce and how much money we can get for this, we then lose sight of the value of trees to our environment.

I make this point in order to underline the fact that we are all being shaped by the market value. If we are to reconstruct society, based on basic values, if we are to move away from knowing the price of everything and the value of nothing, we must obviously begin with ourselves and then move on to institutions and organisations. If we're serious about it, we need to develop workable partnerships.

FS: *The EU Leader programme looks like a step in that direction.*

HB: It is and it's something that should be welcomed. I am involved with Rural Resources Development (RRD) Ltd. in County Clare, a partnership of statutory, private sector and voluntary sector bodies operating through the Leader programme. RRD supports over 100 small economic projects around the county, all of which are driven by local people in the interests of the local area.

I really like the way this programme empowers people to do things for themselves. You have local initiatives with public and/or private funding with expertise as a back-up resource rather than a prime mover. It breaks that dependence that became a hallmark of investment in the past but it also initiates a process of empowerment that begins and ends with respect.

FS: *In capitalist ideology, the market will take care of itself.*

HB: That's the thinking, but it does raise this issue of market value. It's a key element that has to be addressed. Our position is that market value has become so powerful and so literal that people at the very heart of it are those who are productive. People at either end, whether it's children or elderly or sick, are becoming less and less valued.

Just take the health service, for example. We have long waiting lists for those who cannot afford health insurance. Isn't it appalling that this can happen in a society which now ranks among the 20 wealthiest countries in the world?

There are huge warning signs that we cannot continue to ignore. When market values become so dominant that they penetrate into areas of society where they do not properly belong, we then begin to have massive social problems. Market values do not properly belong in the areas of medicine and law and yet we have all the signs that they are becoming central to these professions.

It's so pervasive that they begin to influence our decisions on how to treat our elderly, or, as I mentioned earlier, whether couples will buy a new car or have a new baby! Maybe only then do we start to see how these values have begun to influence social, political and commercial behaviour in a dangerous way. Of course, the market will take care of itself. But a global or national economy is not a global or national society.

Part Three

New Foundations

FS: *What do you find appealing about the credit union movement?*

HB: I particularly like its ethos of democracy and social responsibility. It's really a continuation of the ideals and beliefs that prompted the agricultural co-operative movement insofar as it shares the goal of human and social development. Credit unions possess a vision of social justice that extends both to the individual members and to the larger community in which they work and reside. The ideal is to extend service to all who need it and can use it. Everyone is a potential member and thus falls within the credit union's sphere of interest and concern.

FS: *How have credit unions survived?*

HB: They've done better than that — they have thrived. I think it's because people need the service, they feel they have a personal stake in it insofar as the credit union represents a true sense of community. You know, it's quite telling that in a profit-driven age full of "*mé féin*" attitudes, the credit union movement upholds its original premise. It continues to provide a service that measures favourably against these basic principles.

The movement has not been swayed by economic changes. Credit unions are not established to make a profit. They are totally member-focused, as opposed to the profit-led shareholder concerns of a conventional bank.

There are many wonderful examples of a local credit union branch interacting with its community. The members of St Columba's branch in Galway, for example, were asked to set up an enterprise centre in a deprived area of Galway. The Board of Directors saw this as a unique opportunity of continuing the ideals and beliefs of its founders, so they got involved.

The future challenge for credit unions might be to invest more in the whole concept of community and Céifin is currently in discussions on the idea of partnerships to bring this about.

But we can look at other areas too in the non-profit sector. No one should underestimate its economic power — in 1995, non-profit enterprises were worth around €4 billion in expenditure alone. Without them, many of the services provided in Ireland would simply fold — including voluntary hospitals, sports organisations, community developments, social services, environmental, arts and cultural organisations. Collectively, the voluntary sector is a heavy-hitter and just because its businesses aren't run for profit, it would be a serious mistake to underestimate their worth. The same goes for credit unions.

FS: *Certainly the growth of the voluntary sector has been remarkable.*

HB: Well it's not too surprising when voluntarism is, increasingly, the only option. I think the western world realised some time ago that many of the social problems we now face will not be solved by economic growth. Many services that began within the voluntary sector have become a vital ancillary arm of mainstream economics. The welfare system appears to be fighting a losing battle so I would see an expanding role for participatory programmes.

The anthropologist Margaret Mead said,

> "If you look closely you will see that almost anything that embodies our deepest commitment to the way human lives should be lived and cared for depends on some form — often many forms — of voluntarism."

Dr Mary Redmond, founder of the Irish Hospice Foundation, described the voluntary sector as a "new authority". Speaking at our conference three years ago, she said:

> "The wheel of voluntarism is yet unturned. Think of how powerful it will be when it is turning, its spokes accommodating the rich diversity of the voluntary sector, its centre the distillation of the great energy which drives it."

I think that's a great image. I also think — and hope with this growth — that the ethos of voluntarism can have a humanising effect on the marketplace. The downside, however, is that in a prosperous society fewer people will volunteer their time and energy. Through the 1990s, voluntarism in Ireland fell from 39 per cent of the population to 33 per cent. We can't take any of this for granted.

FS: *Education falls within the remit of the relevant State department, represented at local level by schools. At structural level, it is a top-down, authoritarian, centralised model. If we place the state as one of those monolithic institutions currently in crisis, what hope is there that new generations will learn different ways?*

HB: I'm not quite sure how to tackle the structural inadequacies of the education system but change should come from the ground up. The schools issue has to be addressed quite seriously. Firstly, we need to establish what schools are for.

We should be asking government what role the school actually plays within the community. Is it only part of the economic community or is it part of the wider community? How does the school connect with the environment?

If we were addressing the issues like this, we would have them within school curricula but we don't. Everything we have in schools and universities at the moment is geared towards feeding the economy, but not feeding society. For example, we don't even have citizen responsibility programmes in our schools. Imagine — building a society without a programme like that!?

Against that, we have every sort of course imaginable relating to technology and computers. In other words, we are investing seriously — and rightly so — in the economy but we are now challenged to invest in a school programme that links young people to their own environment — socially, culturally, economically.

FS: *How might these developments change the nature of schooling?*

HB: In a huge way. The schools themselves are backed into a kind of corner. Work has become so central to modern life that parents choose — or are forced — to look for employment. And the effect of this? What I'm hearing over and over again from talks around the country is that teachers have more and more responsibility thrust on them. This is a major issue.

This has placed huge demands on teachers and it's really bewildering for them trying to juggle their new role. The fact that teachers are very competent, committed and generally excellent in what they do is no longer the issue. What it means is that parents are extracting themselves further and further from the process. In the long term, teachers' frustration is going to be highly detrimental to themselves, to the kids and for what schools can achieve.

FS: *So you would like to see the school contribute in a social-educational rather than purely academic sense?*

HB: We're talking about primary schools. Children! I don't think it builds a sense of community when kids are streamlined into groups of similar social background and similar aptitude. If we lose diversity at this stage of experience we lose an important part of the socialisation process.

In Ireland, most schools are under the trusteeship of the Catholic Church. With diminishing numbers of religious, there are major issues about the ongoing management of the school, about the school and the community and about the ethos of schools. These questions apply equally well to secondary schools. We have to understand what we mean by "ethos" and why it is important and think through the values that inform that.

School Development Planning is now a legal requirement but we need to influence that process. Let's start with ideas of community and with the widest possible representation actively choosing what values they want schools to promote.

FS: *Can you put on your sociologist's hat to give us a broader picture of the importance of early school days?*

HB: After family, the school is the second encounter any of us have with the idea of being in a community. Having learned the basic idea of "others", the primary school continues that socialisation process. It is also where we first learn to communicate, orally, in writing and numerically and to get the context of the world around us.

Ideally, all children should leave primary school feeling good about themselves, confident to take the next step and with embryonic values of caring and co-operation. In reality, our primary school system has become quite competitive. Parents want "the best" for their child and that's perfectly understandable.

However, big questions need to be asked when "the best" translates into issues of academic ability and social class. It happens when a ranking system based on academic results is applied as a variable for acceptance to secondary school. We also find schools becoming segregated homogenously rather than having a social mix. That adds to disadvantage of the marginalised and vulnerable in society and I'd also see it as a serious loss to the wider community.

FS: *How do you see the school's role change at secondary level?*

HB: In second-level education, the world of learning broadens. It should be a journey of discovery but at times we are very hide-bound by a restrictive curriculum. Teachers are over-burdened with assessment and paperwork and constrained by curricula.

However, perhaps the single biggest problem is that the role of the teacher and school has changed in relationship to the role of the parent and home. With both parents working and caught up in the pace of everyday life, the teacher is often put in the position of having to act as social worker and deal with numerous social problems. This is over and beyond the role they trained for and places a great deal of stress on the teacher.

The school supervision role is expanding progressively. In many schools there are breakfast clubs or homework clubs, taking on basic responsibilities previously falling within the remit of the family home.

FS: *But for many couples, both partners working is generally a necessity rather than a luxury.*

HB: I fully accept that.

FS: *In fact, the cost of living increases with the arrival of children, exerting even greater pressure to bring home two wage packets.*

HB: People are entitled to work — men and women. It's not for me to say but I think it's a natural thing that if children are brought into the world that somebody rears them from within that scene. Parents should be given the opportunity of doing that. They're not going to be rearing the children forever, so people can work before and after children are born.

There's only a short period of time when children have to be reared, when somebody has to be there for them when they get home from school. I'm not saying it's mother or father but let's say the mother is the most natural of the two rearing kids. If she was accommodated to be at home when the kids were there, I think she could be the best worker that a place could have. I've seen this in places where that flexibility was possible. The mother/parent has got rid of her guilt. She's there when the kids need her and the workplace doesn't tie her, doesn't oblige her to work when she knows her kids are home alone. The human dimension of this working pattern has never been taken into account.

There's a mix of balancing work with family. It's a basic need that needs to be looked at and accommodated. It's established now as a need. We should go forward now and organise in such a way that these things can happen.

FS: *Can we truly look at the education system and say it is the best we can offer?*

HB: Whatever about primary level, secondary school focuses on the Leaving Certificate with an over-emphasis on points for entry to third-level. Teenagers are put under extraordinary pressure by that or by parental expectations and you have additional strain with grinds and so on. Education has been reduced to the points race, the great, late-August spectator sport in Ireland.

Céifin is presently looking at the role of secondary schools as a major resource for the community. This year we will work with ten schools in five counties — Donegal, Clare, Galway, Sligo and Mayo — to assess this role and to explore the values that should underpin the broader approach to a learning community. It's a study I'm particularly interested in following.

FS: *The role of education at primary and secondary levels may be going through its own overhaul but going onto third level is largely a means to an end. Do you accept that the point of studying for a degree or diploma is usually to get a job at the end of it?*

HB: I don't agree that the sole purpose of education should be to satisfy the criteria for some job or other. Third-level education is highly competitive and I think it's become overly vocational. When the CAO applications went in this year, there was near-panic that computer-related courses were under-subscribed, that suddenly the third-level system was failing the future health of the economy.

Somewhere along the line we've lost the concept of education for education's sake. This sort of philosophy only prepares the student to start work and does not give the more lasting educational framework needed to live our lives fully.

Our universities have changed dramatically over the last few decades. Traditionally, they provided a service by critically reflecting on society. Nowadays they are run like businesses with all the emphasis on jobs.

We also see intense competition between universities for research funding and academic recognition. I think this has fostered a sort of race for public merit through high-profile research and publications. It's attention-seeking and to some extent moves education — in its wider sense — further down the line.

There needs to be real thought given to the quality of the learning experience. I would certainly recognise that many universities and colleges are striving to be more open and accessible and to move outside campus walls. That's something I would welcome.

Education is big business but it cannot be run the same as big business. When the heads of universities or colleges see themselves as CEOs, it inevitably creates the wrong ethos and approach. The student becomes either the product or the customer, depending on your point of view, and the whole wealth of learning is lost in a consumerist model. There are major challenges ahead as technology changes the nature of learning. Much thought will have to be given both to the process and to the value system that underpins it.

The balance in education needs to be looked at, between feeding the global economy and maintaining the local culture.

FS: *Considering that all fourteen kids in your own primary school class in Feakle ended up leaving the parish, it's quite understandable that you now stand against school-leavers being ushered quickly towards employment centres.*

HB: Well I have a big problem with any education system that steers people away from their own locality. This also happened in my own time at secondary school where we were encouraged to move on or move out. It was as if the idea of returning home was a step backwards. That sort of thinking can do a lot of damage.

Generations later, we have another version of that. For example, I recently talked to a few students from third-level colleges. They could tell me easily about the whole wide world because travel has become so easy during the summer when they are off. But when I asked them about their own local area they knew very little. So in other words, education seems to be connected much more to the wider world than to the local. That has to be seriously questioned.

FS: *Do you think that spawns an inferiority complex or is it just a case of the other man's grass is always greener?*

HB: I think it has more to do with bending to the sort of pressures exerted by the global mass market. I love hurling but even if I had no time for it, the game had such a tradition in Feakle that our heroes were local hurling heroes you'd see around the place every other day. They weren't some composite televisual image from far away.

The same applies to schools. Some provision is made under the Social and Environmental Programme to study subjects within the unique environs of each school.

The west of Ireland is perfect for this sort of stuff — geography, history, natural studies — but with the exception of highly motivated teachers, schools invariably opt for bland textbooks that cover the country in general. Children miss the opportunity to discover what is special about their own area. Respect and pride must be fostered at school if we are to have any confidence in it.

FS: *But neither hurling nor local studies have a global stage.*

HB: I am absolutely convinced that by focusing on the local, the educational experience can be not only exciting but global in its significance. Are we not more likely to be concerned about the destruction of the rainforest if we're already tuned into the fragile magnificence of The Burren? Or to appreciate the classics if we already appreciate local folk music? Reciprocally, how can we be concerned about the Amazon if we don't care about the Burren? That's what I'm getting at.

FS: *Irish music seems to have survived market pressures, if not benefited from a global reach?*

HB: But we could have lost it. We went very close to discarding Irish music altogether and I would say that one of the great heroes of this country is Cíarán MacMathúna, who recorded Irish music when nobody else wanted to know. He recorded musicians — masters of the fiddle here in Clare — who otherwise would have been forgotten. He kept it alive for other people.

I remember twenty, thirty, forty years ago you'd be almost ashamed to play the fiddle in a public place in Ireland. Now, Irish music is on the world stage. As well as Irish dance.

That's a clear indication to me that if people with pride in their own heritage are given the opportunity on the global stage, they will respond in kind.

FS: *If it went so close to the brink, what explains Irish music now being embraced and revitalised?*

HB: I think that these connections are ingrained in people. We want to identify with the local team, local music, local dance. There's a huge need to identify and we had a huge tradition there within our grasp. Music speaks to the soul.

And that translates into local confidence. The late Miko Russell was one of three musicians who reconstructed folk music around Doolin. Miko and others redefined rural Ireland as a vibrant, sophisticated, artistic and authentic culture. Miko has correctly assumed a symbolic stature in Irish music history not only because of his own genius but because he suggested the possibility of genius at every country crossroads.

People came from all over the world to settle here, adding to the mix, to that growth. Local radio is a huge success here and the airwaves are blooming with Clare accents. That's real change.

FS: *The danger of Irish music — or local culture generally — going global is that it becomes mass-marketed and loses its soul. Are those fears grounded?*

HB: It has been fairly commercialised but I think it will survive comfortably. There will be future masters who will create a commercial market for other musicians to bring Irish music to a wider audience. I think the need for it to retain its soul is there. These things don't stay alive without connecting/reconnecting to the ground.

One of those masters on the world stage is fiddle-player Martin Hayes. He's from near Feakle, my native place, and he's a great friend. Martin comes back here, comes out to our place at home, plays the music, talks to me about where his music comes from — which is where he comes from, the hills around Kilanena. In other words, from his heart and soul. He would play until five o'clock in the morning with the locals and yet two weeks later he could be in concert halls somewhere in Japan or New York.

People like that realise the tradition won't survive without connecting back to its roots. They understand this is where it all came from — the valleys, the hills and the mountains. From a creative people using their own talents.

FS: *We've discussed the major institutions and how they have been caught out by huge social change or actually contributed to it. Does the family in Ireland escape current scrutiny as an institution?*

HB: The changes in the family in Ireland are as radical as changes in any other institution. Probably more so, because changes in the home feed into every facet of our society.

The family in Ireland has moved quickly from the extended family to a nuclear (immediate) family. Not long ago people were brought up not only with a father and mother but also with a granny, uncles, aunts and so on. The extended family was desperately important to the rearing of children and that's why the elderly were highly valued for the role they played.

Then we moved quickly through the nuclear family — in 1980 the nuclear family accounted for only 45 per cent of all households. Single-parent homes made up nine per cent of households.

And the pattern has since changed again, leading us to various definitions of family. Society moves on but I would argue that the constitutional position is deeply flawed.

FS: *Well, according to Article 41 of the Constitution of Ireland, "The State recognises the family as the natural primary and fundamental unit group of society . . . the State, therefore, guarantees to protect the family in its constitution and authority, as the necessary basis of social order as indispensable to the welfare of the Nation and the State." Where's the flaw?*

HB: That's the statutory position — the family as the basic unit of Irish society which must be protected at all costs. But is that state *policy?* No! State policy promotes the techno-logical world, the work-friendly world, so we are actually weakening the family structure all the time. The ties are be-ing constantly loosened.

You can see this on monetary and practical issues — in things as practical as paying people to go out to work but not attempting to reward them for staying at home. Or taxation — why do we not examine the rules that make it financially imperative for both parents to leave home in the morning?

I'm not saying people should stay at home either. What about a closer look at job-sharing? A few days at home, or, certain freedoms to be at home when the kids are at home. In other words, if we were serious about protecting the family as an institution we would already be reorganising work to accommodate family life.

It's the basic unit of society. It gives so much meaning in so many ways, especially to young people. The whole thing of experiencing life together. But let's face it — the family is seriously threatened and undermined by modern trends.

We have supported the work-friendly world and in many ways undermined the family scene for the last number of years. It's a massive subject.

I often celebrate weddings and I always felt that at least commitment was for life. Whether it actually worked out is another thing but when it comes now to vows of lifelong commitment, I have to admit I wouldn't be so sure.

FS: *The pattern of marriage in Ireland has changed significantly since the 1950s. Do the trends disturb you?*

HB: I just wonder about this idea of permanence. Is it an issue? I mean the changes are massive. Back in the '50s, Ireland had the lowest marriage rate in Europe. The average age for marrying was 33 for men and 28 for women. The average age began to drop so that by 1980 it was 27 for men and 24 for women. The pressures on relationships have risen considerably so the net result is we have couples getting married at a younger age and breaking up more frequently than in the past.

Of course, there are indications that this is changing once again. The age at marriage is rising again. For some couples, maybe cohabitation has replaced marriage for a time, if not altogether.

FS: *Even if people want to play an active part in the extended family it would be difficult to make time between getting to and from work, shopping, picking up the kids and the hundreds of ways daily life is exhausted. What are the consequences of so many extra pressures?*

HB: Well there's no doubt that time feels short because we're all running around, chasing our tails. But the impact of this contracting into smaller family units is that there's greater pressure building up.

It brings us back again to the community because all the studies I've read indicate clearly that if the community breaks down — like when the extended family broke down — the nuclear family comes under severe pressure. The three or four things that held people together in the past have been almost reduced to the emotional plane. Which would mean we are expecting a couple to stay together for thirty or forty years without the space or back-up support most couples need. This is the sort of thing I find cropping up in my pastoral work.

When I hear people saying there's so much breakdown in marriage today, I have to say I'm amazed so many married couples are still together. Because there's serious pressure on the nuclear family. Economically, socially, all kinds of ways.

Once we're so focused into our own worlds we don't have an opportunity to reach out. It's in giving we receive. We really need the opportunity to share with other people in a natural way, not a forced way. Without community, the nuclear family is seriously tested. I don't mean neighbours looking into your back garden. I mean some kind of linking up with other people.

A student from UCG told a Céifin conference two years ago it is urgent and important that children be given back their innocence. The media plays a huge role in taking it away. Advertising targets even the youngest child as a potential consumer and introduces the "I want" culture. This is the Information Age but there's such an onslaught of information and entertainment, children are not getting time to grow up.

I'm hearing more and more parents say that now. I suppose all of that indicates that change is so fast that they need to understand it. And secondly, they need to understand values that make sense out of life. I think that's a fundamental thing that's emerging for us.

FS: *The extended family may well be in decline but is that the only change that makes parenting more difficult?*

HB: No, but it is a major factor. Obviously this is not in my own experience but what I see over and over again is the strain brought about because of the speed of social change. There has been so much disconnecting from the institutions of the past, we are now left with a vacuum and indeed a lot of confusion.

FS: *Is this not the case all over the world?*

HB: It is a worldwide phenomenon but like I said, it happened in one generation for us. The extended family is almost gone and now we're into a very short period of the nuclear family. I can remember McInerneys building the first private housing estate in Ireland in Caherdavin, Limerick. That's only 40 years ago. These houses would have been advertised with the fine-looking couple with the two kids and the car outside on the driveway. That was the nuclear family and I remember being captivated by that image and how — or why — this was the new ideal.

It seemed to me that the nuclear family could come under serious pressure if life was organised in such a way that the partners had so little time for sharing together, and yet their togetherness depended very heavily on sharing time with one another — much more than in the past when couples on farms shared work, prayer, rearing children, taught them skills and so on.

The key is that the family is the basic unit of our society. It is critical to so many aspects of life that we need to be careful to provide every support needed to sustain it. Is it fair to demand so much of the nuclear family without the support of a wider community interest? I don't think so. Yet the current mode of working and living, where everything is subservient to and seen in terms of economics, expects the nuclear family to "take up the slack". These are the pressures that are put on relationships and families, and are causing so much pain and hardship through marital breakdown, depression and even suicide.

This doesn't mean the extended family of the past was perfect but there was a whole support system in place, not just in times of crisis but for routine, everyday living. There was a whole interlinking with nature as against living in concrete jungles. We saw this first-hand when we started the rural housing scheme. The idea was to revitalise village communities which in turn serviced a hinterland. This was very much part of the settlement pattern in Ireland. The idea was based on the systems of family and community, the two systems that held Irish society together for generations.

If society is genuinely concerned about balanced living, then high-rise flats and massive housing estates are not the answer. On the face of it, economics may demand that housing people in this kind of way solves the numbers problem. It may solve an accommodation problem but I don't think people were ever intended to live in high-rise flats.

A hundred years after the industrial revolution in Britain, it was shown not to be the answer. I saw it myself during my studies there on the growth of cities in the 1960s. Planning went full-circle from high-rise flats to housing estates to new towns. That was back then. I saw the most beautiful block of flats going up in Liverpool but it lasted only 25 years and then had to be pulled down. I came back here and what did I see? High-rise flats going up in Dublin. We didn't seem to learn from their mistakes.

FS: *Given that you were guided by concepts of family and community, did the Rural Housing Organisation offer anything different?*

HB: We carried out a study ten years after setting up and found that a whole web of social organisations had sprung up among people who got involved in the scheme. They didn't feel imprisoned in some vast, anonymous estate. They brought new life to sporting and cultural organisations. They identified with neighbours and they were connected to the natural environment. They felt all of this made a big difference to their lives.

FS: *Was the essential purpose of the RHO to offer local people who lived at home a chance to stay?*

HB: Yes — and to encourage them to stay. When I returned to Feakle from Britain in 1972, the village had a population of 120 people. Only three were aged between 20 and 40, even though we were within 20 miles of Ennis, Shannon and Limerick.

Everybody was still moving out. I was absolutely convinced that we could make it work so, despite advice to the contrary, I borrowed £1,500 from the bank manager Johnny Mee and organised an action group. Johnny himself joined up, which was a great boost.

The way it was, rural areas were seen merely as suppliers of labour to growth centres. Our small towns and villages were completely neglected in a systematic policy of diverting national resources away from small communities. It's as though all local endeavour had to go off and fit into some grand design, much of it dependent on multinationals setting up in Ireland.

Foreign investment was very welcome but we failed to plan our settlements and so relied on the provision of housing with little or no reference to the concept of community.

Unfortunately, many of our working class housing estates which sprung up in the '60s quickly turned into unemployment blackspots with serious social consequences. We were draining existing communities of life and creating an artificial environment. We could have been far more imaginative.

We discovered that, given an opportunity, many young people had the capacity for highly productive self-sufficiency and indeed for starting up their own businesses. Thus creating employment for themselves and for others. We felt we needed to develop that. The challenge was less to create potential than to release it.

FS: *But most jobs are in and around cities which makes urbanisation almost inevitable. If we wanted to reverse that trend, what aspects of the rural development scheme might be applied?*

HB: I believe there is a strong case to be made in this Information Age to bring work close to people rather than the other way round. The way technology has developed, we don't need big centralised models any more.

People are stretched by the current system, whether it's the stress of getting the kids out to school, commuting to work, paying for crèche facilities — which are exorbitant and very scarce — and then doing the same in reverse every evening, getting home, picking up the kids, shopping, cooking dinner. No wonder people are getting burnt out.

I fully understand that many people like to get out of the house to go to work and for them the social aspect of work is very important. The point is, it doesn't suit everybody and we need to look at alternatives. We could review the system that worked in pre-industrial times to see if aspects of it could be applied today. It might mean locating workplaces in smaller towns and villages rather than putting everything into cities.

I firmly believe we could reorganise employment centres in a much better way and link them to spatial planning. There are a number of towns in each county which could be developed around employment opportunities rather than diverting almost everything to already over-populated stretches of the east coast.

For example, last year Intel announced another thousand jobs for its Leixlip plant. I'm quite sure Leixlip needed an extra thousand jobs like a hole in the head because of pressures on the infrastructure, housing, environment and so on. But Kilrush in County Clare could have done with it!

In the 1980s, when the economy took a downturn, a new energy emerged at local level in Ireland. People took the initiative to come together to create a new future for themselves and their children.

It's no coincidence that when Mary Robinson made her inaugural speech as President of Ireland in 1990, she remarked, "I have found local community groups thriving on a new sense of self-confidence and self-empowerment at work." Now that our economy is experiencing another blip, people may be forced to return to their own resources.

However, we must find a better way of planning our settlements for the future. It is inconceivable that nearly half the population of a small island could be concentrated around the capital city. Over a quarter of a century ago, it was evident that there were massive dangers involved in this. Hopefully, the experience of congestion, pollution, crime will force us to pause and plan our future in a much more imaginative way.

FS: *The demographic concentration in Dublin has created huge problems. Ironically, however, you can hit a traffic jam in every medium-sized town in the country, including here in Shannon!*

HB: I know. Many features of life that apply to urban living also apply at county level. There is every opportunity for more effective planning.

Indeed, each of us has a responsibility to play our part in solving some of our problems. Even if we consider how the car has come to monopolise our lives.

Recently, I was driving from Shannon to Ennis at 7.30 a.m. and the cars coming against me were bumper-to-bumper on their way to work. I made a mental calculation that for every 20 cars, about 19 carried just the driver.

Fifteen years ago it would have been the opposite. Every car would have brought about four people. Since then, wealth and individualism have become a powerful combination and it's difficult to counter that, even when people are stuck in traffic jams every day. The simple truth is, we could reduce both congestion and pollution through car-sharing, and even get to know each other a bit better.

Mobility became a reality in Ireland with the car. We could still turn that to our advantage by distributing employment centres around the country instead of loading everything around gridlocked Dublin.

FS: *Do you feel the Rural Housing Scheme proved itself?*

HB: I think it did. As a voluntary organisation, we built 2,500 houses in 120 villages from Cavan to Cork. People were given the opportunity of living where they wanted to and the spin-off benefits have been very significant. Schools and shops came back to life, and often expanded. Young parents brought a balance to the age structure of the population. People started up their own businesses.

It could have led to many more major developments. For example, I saw then the opportunity of setting up a bank — whereby, sticking with the idea of the German people's bank, money deposited in an area would be reinvested in that area. I still believe this concept should be explored.

FS: *If the rural housing scheme was so good, why was it not replicated all over the country?*

HB: We met with a lot of opposition, as indeed most significant community initiatives did. Government was so all-powerful it was very important that people would be made to feel dependent on it.

That same dependency was very important to the political representative system. Once people started to take initiatives themselves, power was moving towards the ordinary people and by definition this meant away from the political system. And so, I believe, it was resented.

When we started out, everybody in officialdom told us the idea would never work. We said it could. The people who took up the scheme lived where they wanted to live. The scheme proved itself.

Sometimes I think if officialdom could have entered a partnership with people on a movement of this kind, a whole new approach to development could have taken place. Unfortunately, we were not conditioned then to work in this kind of way. Hopefully, a strong communitarian movement will at least move us forward in the direction of working in partnership.

FS: *The Céifin approach seems like a cross between a think-tank and a pressure group. Many of the issues you are raising here pertain to political, social and economic life in Ireland. By its nature, Céifin stands outside the system, looking in.*

HB: I wouldn't agree with that assessment. Céifin is deliberately independent and objective but we're operating very much *within* the political system. What we call democracy is *representative* democracy. We elect people to represent us.

What I'm saying is that real democracy is *participative*. Eventually, I would love to see our political leaders emerging from the participants within the community so they will actually represent the concerns of local people and communities. People have to get involved, to participate instead of waiting passively for some person or organisation to sort out the problems. It's an ideal but it's the only one I believe will make any sense if we're going to restore the balance.

FS: *Why not set up a new political party to articulate the same concerns and work within the established system?*

HB: That's not what Céifin is about. There are enough political parties and as far as we're concerned, participative democracy is the way to go.

What I believe is people now want to participate more in determining their own future. The self-interest of powerful political, religious and economic institutions did not allow that in the past.

Now, if people want to participate in their own future, you're talking about participative democracy in each of these institutions. In the Catholic Church, for example, it would mean de-clericisation. People would own and control their Church. You'd still have priests of course but in a different role altogether. Their role would be spiritual but a lot of the things priests do today would be done by the people.

It's the same in politics. In other words, people who would be elected would come from within the community, would be participating in the community and would be answering to a structure within the community.

FS: *Recent general elections have produced a growing number of independent TDs. Is that something you would welcome — constituencies voting for national representatives on the basis of local issues?*

HB: I think that highlights a fairly serious vacuum in the party political system. I mean, the political system is there for people to use and it's better that people are engaged rather than apathetic, whether they are drawn in by local or national issues.

FS: *Surely most local issues can be dealt with by local government?*

HB: In theory, yes, but I don't think that's how it works in practice. The alienation of Irish people from government is common to both central and local government. Indeed, I would suggest that in many ways this constitutes a significant threat to democracy.

If we examine the structures of decision-making, we find that a few experts, administrators and politicians dictate what kind of society we should have without any participatory role for the people. And of course, when the interests of politics and big business merged substantially, people in power forgot what they were about, ultimately leading to serious problems for both.

Participation is not an optional extra any more. Ordinary people will demand their right to participate in their future. The most effective form can be at local level.

FS: *Misgivings about local authority seems to have lasted for some time, even back to when Muintir na Tire was set up.*

HB: Canon John Hayes established Muintir na Tire in the 1930s and you'd have to say that its original ideals ring a bell:

> "to promote the practical application of those Christian principles that pertain to social, educational and economic problems; to attain a higher and more uniform standard of living, and a more uniform standard of income and spending, and to direct the entire life of the nation along Christian, national, non-party lines."

Whatever those aspirations, it's probably an indication of how people avoided, even back then, the local institution that was supposed to serve the community. Muintir na Tire's 1943 handbook reads:

> "It was disappointing . . . to come across so many who had not grasped the meaning and aims of Muintir na Tire. What did it propose to do — to build rural halls? To promote rural amusements? To make roads, to sink pumps? Muintir na Tire proposes to do none of these things, although, in fact, it may hope to be effective in getting any or all of them done."

Canon Hayes deserves a lot of credit for tackling the dominant institutional ethos of the day. Muintir na Tire's approach is outdated but more ominously, those institutions are still in place and the conditions his organisation wanted to address are disturbingly familiar.

FS: *A general decline in voting figures would suggest that apathy is spreading among the electorate.*

HB: There's no doubt about it. We could ignore it but within that sense of alienation lies a serious threat to the system of democracy. If people don't believe in the structures that are supposed to run the country at local and national level, where does that lead to?

A few years back, I was struck by what happened in the dairy co-operatives. An enterprise that started as a great success — farmers were democratically involved as members, owners and managers — came to grief unbelievably quickly. Despite the co-ops' success, farmers dropped out overnight. It was clear to me that they not only lost confidence in what purported to be a democratic institution but they actually felt a powerful sense of hostility towards the co-ops afterwards.

What it tells us is that an enterprise or government which fails to engage the energy, goodwill and collective enthusiasm of the people can jeopardise the principles of — and belief in — democracy itself. This has broader implications when we look at other areas where people experience extreme disillusionment in democratic institutions.

FS: *How can this alienation be addressed?*

HB: Alienation is the response to a form of disempowerment. I believe it's a condition, not just an inability to effect change but also a condition of oppression. It's an important distinction because alienation is not simply passivity as it's often taken for. There is a feeling that power is not just absent but has been taken away.

In *Pedagogy of the Oppressed*, Paolo Freire wrote that the process of empowerment involves the removal of sources of oppression. Participation is the antithesis to alienation but people are only going to participate in systems that don't shut them out. By getting people involved, the contribution of participants is acknowledged and validated. People can see they make a difference instead of feeling lost and disempowered at the end of the line.

I don't want to get unrealistic here but the first steps towards solving our long-term difficulties will involve the reorganisation of the state and raising the quality of life by forging a sense of community.

A massive gap has been created between those at the top and the person on the ground. Frequently, we see top executives picking up massive bonuses as a result of a company's share performance. What are the rewards for people who promote and foster human rights? This is a question I believe will have to be addressed if the balance between social and economic development is to be restored.

FS: *Do you think that the spate of tribunals, this "confronting history", will clear the way for a better system? Or maybe that's wishful thinking.*

HB: So many things have come crashing down we have almost been anaesthetised from the wider issue of ethics. If we are confronting our history, we have to be extremely careful that it leads to significant change. After so much self-examination, things can't just go on in the manner that got us into this mess.

Otherwise ethics will be permanently devalued. Why bother tell the truth when it pays to lie? Should we respect people who take an oath, testify and then lie to save their skins? If these people remain as "pillars of society" it tells all of us that honesty has no value. It tells us success is what gains public respect. And money is a reliable barometer of success within the present system. In a way this is how money has supplanted intrinsic values like honesty and integrity.

I think we're going to have to start trying to discover what truth is and building up trust again. People like Mary Robinson have been calling for a new ethic for a world order. I think if we could start working at restoring the balance in Ireland, the communitarian message will be picked up elsewhere because this is something of international significance.

International borders are not a boundary on this stuff. Earlier this summer, we had 50 black South Africans with us for a fortnight to see how we got involved in developing rural communities. The demonstration effect works. We've had people right across the developing world coming here to experience what we are doing and see how some of our ideas can be transferred to their communities.

FS: *If we are now entering a post-industrial age, is it coincidental that we may also enter a post-institutional age?*

HB: I'm not sure if it's coincidental but institutions do literally have to be re-formed. That's why the communitarian movement has to be much more than a cosy little thing at ground level. It has to be a strong people's movement. We have to find a voice and use that voice to identify issues concerning institutions that continue to be unjust.

Once we start into the new model of community, the Church and other institutions will have to respond. That's where Ireland is now. All institutions must be challenged. In the context of great power out there in the financial markets, the reformation of institutions that have been powerful in the past will involve a working partnership with the people and with other organisations. The current system is not working and the established institutions cannot work as autonomous powers any more. Betrayal has left its mark.

I'm disappointed but not hugely surprised when I hear adults, teachers, trainers of sporting teams, priests, say they're not able to relate to young people any more. I think we have to do a serious amount of re-thinking. And at the very heart of that has to be the rebuilding of trust. Unless we can work through that ,we're going to suffer very badly.

That's why these decades are critical because all these things are coming to light now. Things are coming to a head in the western world generally — and particularly in Ireland. It's sticking out a mile to me that we have difficult years ahead if we don't stand back a bit and critically analyse what direction we are taking. We need to allow people time and create space to identify the values that are really important and give meaning to their lives.

Part Four

The Need for Values-Led Change

FS: *Maybe at this point we should return to where this discussion began. A woman attending the Ennis conference asked who was going to rear the next generations. Are we any closer to an answer?*

HB: I think the answer must come from listening to people and re-forming social organisations. We need to devise a new model for society whereby people come together to identify what's important for them. They must be encouraged to improve the situation and empowered to make it happen.

FS: *Essentially we're talking about society helping itself, encouraging people to participate in effecting positive change and getting life back in balance. How can Céifin help the situation?*

HB: Céifin has begun to provide the opportunity both for the individual and institution people to identify:

- what we are forgetting
- how we can work towards balance
- how we might redefine roles and relationships

how we take responsibility, based on values

- how we can each make a difference.

We are setting up branches around the country to afford people the opportunity to clarify their values, identify what leadership means, create space for conversation, all activities that will lead to personal, organisational and societal change.

FS: *Is society ready for this?*

HB: We have to be. Otherwise society is heading for a major crisis — if we haven't already got there.

Actually I think a lot of this boils down to the fact that our generation and generations before us were shaped by a world of institutions and big organisations. It was the age of the organisation. Whatever institution we belonged to monopolised our lives for the most part. They were free from competition; no checks, no accountability. They all worked well in a stable, predictable environment. They generated loyalty, provided a career for life. In return they expected obedience, respect for seniors and acceptance that the organisation knows best.

One thing we have all learned toward the end of the 20th century is that centrally planned systems don't work. However, while the old system of institution may have gone forever, organisations will still be needed. The point is, they will need to be very different.

Indeed these are dangerous times for big organisations unless they reform. They face a number of major challenges:

- how to remain big and even grow but remain small and personal

- how to combine creativity and efficiency

- how to be prosperous but socially acceptable

- how to reward the owners of ideas as well as the owners of the company.

In short, the future will be about the responsibility of the
individual and about new forms of community.

FS: *How might this come about?*

HB: Change happens when a lot of people do things differently. A lot will depend on individual initiative but Céifin can
give direction to both individuals and groups.

We would anticipate a sea-change ahead when Céifin
branches emerge around the country, each doing something
differently in their workplace, community, organisation or
wherever. Céifin will facilitate this at local level, providing
workshops around the concept of change, facilitating debate
through the conferences, feeding to policy-makers and so on.

All of this underlines the fact that the reconstruction of
society will take place from the ground up and that is the
era we are now in.

FS: *You sound very optimistic about its prospects.*

HB: I really am — and with good reason. If we go back to
the starting question, it's doesn't surprise me that concerns
expressed a few years ago are still unresolved.

For instance, at a recent meeting to establish a Céifin
branch in Galway, participants were asked to identify the key
issue facing our society. After reflection and dialogue, this
was identified as the importance of allowing young people to
grow up. The reason given for this was because everything
else emanates from this, whether it's parenting, work, life-
styles — everything.

And to back up that type of work on the ground, we have just completed a study on work-lifestyles with clinical psychologist Dr Miriam Moore. We found that almost two-thirds of the adult sample said that neither they nor their partners are at home when their children return from school.

FS: *Can you specify how the work/home, parent/child dynamic has changed?*

HB: I would say that the change has been profound. It's also par for the course. Many of the responses in our study are very revealing. Typically, you'd have a parent saying, "I would avail of term-time and other family-friendly hours but it would mean a cut in income and the family couldn't afford that", or "Women who go on the 'mommy track' are not taken seriously and don't get promoted".

There is also a widespread feeling, particularly among working mothers, that it is inappropriate to let management know about having responsibilities/concerns/worries outside work. As though it is a sign of weakness or distraction. One woman told the survey, "We have to leave our humanity and our children at the gate when we go to work."

I just wonder what sort of society creates pressure like this? No matter how materially successful we become, we are failures if we ignore the emotional needs of our children. Endless sociological studies show us that if we do that we lay the foundation for future depression, suicides, criminality and impaired relationships.

FS: *But the flexitime idea does not suit every type of job. Having children and pursuing a career usually means a sacrifice somewhere along the line.*

HB: Yes, but the sacrifice is always made at the children's expense. And long term, that's where we're getting it wrong.

I realise there's a delicate mix to balancing work with family. But look, we provide low-cost university education for young adults and that's the way it should be. We need to give the same priority to ensuring a secure, emotional foundation at the beginning of the lives of infants and young children. This requires the same level of investment.

It's a basic need that arises in real life and, as such, it has to be looked at and accommodated. We should move forward now and make it possible for these things to happen.

And that's just discussing one aspect of where we are. So when we say we want Céifin to become a real force within Irish society, when we say we need serious investment now in community, in relationships and the things that give meaning to life, we are underlining the need for a radical movement which puts people at its centre. This cannot happen by wishing it to happen. It will take serious investment and real commitment — intellectually, socially, financially — to bring it about.

Allied to other efforts, it will mean a participative democracy, a collaborative Church and a business world that moves closer and closer to the co-operative idea. That's what we're aiming for. It also means that some things have to die so that something else comes alive.

FS: *Social change swept across Ireland remarkably quickly but at this stage what began in the early '90s has been happening for over ten years. Much of this transformation has passed through without a murmur of protest. Why do you think there's a growing disquiet with the way things are heading?*

HB: It's down to a realisation of the kind of lives we're creating for ourselves. We're getting used to a pace of life that leaves no time for us to step off the treadmill. We spend so much time hurrying to and from work, for example, and there's this constant pressure on our time. We've also reached an unprecedented level of outside influence, a virtual bombardment of news and information from the global mass media into our homes, pubs, even our cars. I think people are reaching their limits.

FS: *You talk about some of the things modernity brings us, whether we want them or not. What have we lost?*

HB: Time! We don't seem to have time — or allow for time — to reflect on what matters most to us. We've also lost contact, especially with the elderly. The rise of television as an authority figure has been one of the most subtle and significant changes since the 1970s and although this is a worldwide phenomenon, many children know more about MTV singers, chat show hosts, actors and actresses than they do about their own grandparents.

These things hit home and adjusting to influences like these isn't easy for parents who grew up in such a different environment. For example, last year I went to a meeting of about twenty people to discuss local issues. Over the years when I was involved in the Rural Redevelopment Programme, we used to have meetings like this all the time. I got used to that sort of exchange, talking about houses, just easy practical stuff. This particular evening I just thought we could move into different areas. After about half an hour I said to them, I'd love to sit in a circle and discuss the things that are really important to you. And this is what we did. We sat around and talked for nearly three hours, with each person getting around to articulating what mattered to them. It's not as if they had ready answers but once the debate opened up it was great what insights people could bring to it.

You'd have parents saying something like they found it difficult rearing children. Or how embarrassed they'd feel not knowing the answers to all the questions kids were now asking. In one generation their children were growing up into a different world and the parents weren't so sure of their footing. These adults felt they never got an opportunity to debate that with other people. That was a major issue.

FS: *It sounds like it was a very honest, open discussion.*

HB: It was — when we called it a night, several people said to me that was the best night they'd had for years. I think it was because they got a chance to consider what matters to them and to contribute to an honest, open debate.

One man said, "Isn't this great — just to be able to sit around having a chat with neighbours about the things which really concern us. And it helps to share."

We're all conditioned to tune into the box or into other people talking about affairs that affect us. People are expected or conditioned to be passive and they're not given the opportunity to participate in the issues that most affect them. This has to change.

We found a different dynamic that night. We searched together, identifying the things that were really important to them. This was just an ordinary night with a group of ordinary people but the search itself had its own merits. And when we broke through to the heart of it, a lot of things we ended up talking about centred around values.

FS: *How is that significant?*

HB: I think it's very significant. I mean, often we get caught up with financial concerns but none of these people had a major problem with money. They weren't wealthy but they didn't feel that money was their biggest problem. As far as they were concerned if we keep spending it on luxuries and don't have time to spend on one another, it won't matter how much money is in our pockets. We'll never have enough.

Instead of needing a lot of money every time you want to go out, you could have a conversation. That's cheap and comes for nothing. The richness of it is in the sharing.

I believe we have to facilitate people to identify their real concerns. We assume they only want success. We assume we know what people want — as consumers, in careers. Of course, there are things people want and things people are being driven towards but we need to get beyond that. I think you'd be surprised that people's real concerns are often simpler and more profound than a new car, a new house or promotion at work.

FS: *If our lives are getting increasingly distracted by side issues and consumerism, how do we pare things down to core values?*

HB: Sometimes I think core values are so obvious to us that often we don't even realise it! Maybe that's partly because we don't allow ourselves time to reflect on these things.

Even when we look at economic performance, we measure the success of the economy here in terms of GDP and GNP. But as Robert Kennedy said, these things don't measure how happy or how secure young people are. Or what family life is like. Or how communities have been torn apart by drugs and why.

What I'm saying in many ways is that the search for meaning, for well-being, has never been greater in Ireland. But I'm also saying we have a great opportunity to search for this in Ireland. Just as we gave in the past other messages to Europe and to the whole world, I think our major contribution to Europe — and indeed to the western world — could be within that search. It's not just Ireland could do with this. There's a worldwide need for it now, this quest people have for sharing lives with one another.

We have to get away from this idea of people being passive. Of telling them what they want. We have to start listening because there is a need out there to let people speak for themselves.

FS: *Do people know what they want?*

HB: I think that people need time and a bit of space to get back to discovering what they want. It's not always obvious straight away but in the right conditions we can cut through the many distractions of modern life to get to core values.

What we're aiming to do is to try to identify values that are important to us. To help us understand change. We do this through listening to people. Debating the issues. Search and research. Listening to people on the ground as against listening to gurus — wherever they come from — and what you invariably discover is different messages start coming back. The needs out there are very different to what the world is telling people they need.

Take that group meeting, for example. Listening to people that night convinced me — if I ever needed convincing — that institutions can only communicate to people if they know what concerns people on the ground. We have to step away from broadcasting in one direction. We really need to listen.

FS: *When you refer to values-led change, you speak in terms of community. As we've discovered, the definition of community is changing all the time. Why does it remain so central to your thinking?*

HB: When I think of community I think of people and the way people live. Now it is absolutely true that the meaning of community has changed. We could now define it as anything from a small group of people to the European Union. There have to be new definitions and new models.

Furthermore, we need to de-compartmentalise people from gender, occupation, family role, whatever. From my experience, both as a priest and as a sociologist, community is the means to change the way we live. People need people and if the way we live has gone astray, we need to involve people to put us back on course. We want them to be heard.

FS: *And so the search for shared values?*

HB: That's it. I see values or ethics as practical rules for living. I have already said but it does bear repeating that when a society experiences major change, there is often a crisis in values and we are experiencing that crisis now. Individual freedom has emerged as the most important value and as a result, relationships have been undermined.

From our work at Céifin, we believe an agreed set of values can only evolve from the ground up. To define those values, we ask a fundamental question: "What is important to you?"

If you put that question to people across the board — the parent, the businessperson, the professional, the individual, the religious, the community leader — it is possible to identify what is common to all. That gives us the basis for shared values.

FS: *What use or purpose do shared values serve?*

HB: They give us guidelines to a vision for the future. We can just go on criticising governments for a lack of vision but that's not going to get us anywhere. Besides, they've nothing to go on if they don't tap into — or indeed facilitate identifying — an agreed set of values.

Without that sort of vigorous consultation with people, governments and institutions become more and more distant from the people. And isn't this part of the problem? The only qualitative measures to hand are crude yardsticks like GNP or consumer indexes.

Shared values offer the blueprint for the future direction of society. Values are not always comfortable. Sharing, honesty, ethical judgements are not the easy road and we have got too used to the easy road.

FS: *Do people ever tell you this is pie in the sky?*

HB: People are really searching for answers. There is serious confusion out there. We're trying to address that confusion.

It's not surprising some people would dismiss what we are doing. You know, we're living in a pragmatic society where the idea of shared values appears impractical. Values might be seen as the legacy of a religious tradition adapted for modern society but I think right now we're operating in the dark.

We need a set of shared values to create a link between our basic assumptions and our behaviour. Instead, we have a set of laws and "rights". These need to be imposed and enforced because they don't come *from* the community. In practice, laws and rights are not nearly as effective as values in bringing the community together.

FS: *But is the community quite so unified?*

HB: From the feedback we're getting, there is no question that the more serious issues concern people everywhere.

Between the Rural Development Programme and Céifin I have been involved in assessing social change for about 30 years. When we held our first conference, "Are We Forgetting Something?", we brought together quite a cross-section of Irish society. I realised immediately we had touched on something. That people felt something was missing from their lives. Economic success was provoking new and very penetrating questions and speakers at the conference were expressing the very concerns all of us have begun to sense.

FS: *The idea of a community movement — is it compatible with individual freedom?*

HB: It's totally compatible with the freedom of the individual. Besides, freedom isn't real freedom if it's only about self-interest. True freedom comes from sharing with fellow human beings. It gives meaning to life and can only be attained when people genuinely share life with one another.

FS: *How do you translate the communitarian model into a national movement?*

HB: It's quite simple really. We made up our minds after our first conference in Ennis that we wouldn't allow it to become just a talk-shop, that we'd go out and do something about it. We set up a programme of action but we were surprised to find that the debate had already gathered a momentum of its own.

New groupings were forming around the country. They were — and are — springing up because people asked — and are asking — to have them. It's not us just setting up a network. It's the need that is driving the demand. Céifin branches in Waterford and Galway, for example, were set up by people who wanted to forge ahead. We can provide back-up information for these groupings on the basis of debate and research we carry out. That's how the programme is evolving.

FS: *What's the urgency?*

HB: What we are confronting is a crisis — a virtual break-down in society. We have an opportunity, a challenge and an obligation to do something about it.

This isn't reaching back to the past. Whether it's past, present or future, people need to share their lives with other people. To me, that word communitarianism has meaning.

FS: *And that meaning is?*

HB: A new model of community. It's a model of people working together, interlinking around the country into a kind of people's movement. I'm not stuck on this idea of "national movement" as such, because I think the concept of nation-states has become almost irrelevant. Even in political terms, we're talking about the EU, the US, the UN and so on but if we're starting at community level, who's to say how far this can grow?

FS: *Is it anomalous for communitarianism to have global aspirations?*

HB: No, but if it works here it can work anywhere. Why wouldn't it? The demand is worldwide. We have to make a start, be prophetic about this and look ahead. There is no way society can continue the way we are at the moment. It is unthinkable. I think we start at local level and there's no reason to put a ceiling on what we can achieve.

FS: *We talked earlier about the impact of globalisation. From your perspective, is communitarianism the antithesis of globalisation?*

HB: Communitarianism tries to retrieve the ideal of the common good and make it a workable solution. I think it's fairly obvious that the common good has suffered under global capitalism. Even in this year's world summit in Johannesburg, Thabo Mbeki, the President of South Africa, remarked that we now have "islands of wealth in a sea of poverty".

He's absolutely right and geopolitical reality puts the whole concept of communitarianism under threat. Globalisation leads to extreme inequalities between countries and regions, it causes huge population shifts as well as creating political instability and violent conflict. All of this is driven by profit and the common good doesn't get a look in.

FS: *It's often easier to consider the effects of globalisation in the context of developing countries. Does it apply equally to Ireland?*

HB: Very much so. We see in the business world here how corporations are getting bigger and bigger — even, say, in agriculture, the number of dairy cooperatives will probably reduce to just one or two in time to come.

These amalgamations are concentrating power all the time, whereas we would advocate more people participating at policy-making level.

I was thinking recently of a speech Tom McGurk made at one of our conferences. He remarked that the onset of digital broadcasting might mean that we as a country will lose our terrestrial media outputs. That might sound like an in-house debate at a conference but what happens? Within the year you have the whole country up in arms over RTE losing the rights to show Ireland's international soccer matches. The FAI's decision to sell the rights to Rupert Murdoch's Sky TV was made for £7.5 million sterling without taking anything else into account. It's profit before everything.

It's a typical example and really I think it's too late to wait until all these things break open. It doesn't always have to be big issues at national level but we find that local–national–global concerns are interconnected.

This has to become a serious movement to challenge governments, to challenge corporations to think seriously. You have to challenge them to work with you rather than brushing you off with some handout or other.

I feel the time is right for this. I think there's a movement across the world towards this. As we know, the right idea at the wrong time doesn't hit the ground but the right idea at the right time is another matter. And the time is spot-on for this.

That's why we're emphasising the idea of connecting the branches as a network. If any of these groupings were on their own they would be isolated and nobody would hear what they had to say.

This must become a big noise because politically, it's only when a lot of people get together to raise issues of serious concern that the powers-that-be will listen. The momentum we have now is coming from a lot of people and supported by our proposed new Institute — a modern-day University of the people.

FS: *What sort of response do you expect?*

HB: We know the government is listening. We've already met twice with the Taoiseach's office. I'm satisfied that the Taoiseach is committed to Céifin philosophically and I'm hoping the Government will support us in terms of funds. I would say from high-level discussions we've had that whatever progress is made in economics or in the North, there's an awareness among the powers-that-be that people in society remain seriously disconnected from one another. Questions of social capital, of civic responsibility are becoming major issues.

FS: *Does this mean that Céifin is essentially a pressure group?*

HB: No, because it's not a means to an end for us. Pressure groups usually serve their own interests but the ideas we are promoting serve the common good.

Our aim is to start a movement which will give a voice to the people. We're looking to change things from within so that, for example, a managing director who gets involved will effect changes in his company — like organising work in such a way as to allow parents time to rear their children —

to the benefit of all concerned. We're not here to just talk about things; we want action.

FS: *What sets the Céifin approach apart from other thinking?*

HB: Our approach is to move away from compartmentalising society. Seeing people as people rather than using labels. We look at politics, religion, commerce and so on — which are there to serve the well-being of people — but we want these agencies to operate more on a people basis than on institutional terms.

There's obviously a journey to go on that. We're saying we've definitely lost our way in the other direction, gone too much into the institutional world and left people behind.

The reason we've gone as professionally and as deeply into this is because we're saying that just as we needed universities or institutes of technology to drive the Celtic Tiger, we need something of the same magnitude to underpin the communitarian movement of the future.

It's the same thing in terms of values. We're saying this is all about putting people back into the centre. There's no way around it. The challenge facing society is nothing short of a profound spiritual and social transformation. We're being called to wake up to who we really are and what it is we really want.

At last year's conference, one of our speakers said that the next great frontier is not outer space but inner space and this applies to people wherever they are. Céifin will operate on the premise that change driven by values has people at its centre.

Our actions are the result of both a great deal of reflection and widespread consultation. We met with people from universities, religion, law, finance and listened to their views. Every place we heard the same message — "We're in a cocoon and we're not linking up to the real world."

FS: *Institutions exert their own internal pressures but they still need people to run them. Can we put the abuse of power — whether in politics, commerce or the Catholic Church — down to institutional design or is it just a sign of human weakness?*

HB: Naturally we need people to run them but the system is designed in a way to look after itself. For example, the Catholic Church needs to review its diocesan structure and local government needs to be overhauled.

Institutions would be readily accountable if they were responding to people's real concerns. If people were what really counted in the political system, you wouldn't have irresponsible claims being made that hospital waiting lists will be cut within three years. Where is the accountability there?

It wouldn't have to be done like that if we were working off a different model. Institutions need to be restructured. If we could do that, people would be much more willing to do or say things or expose things on the basis of truth.

FS: *Many people might find that a very optimistic view of human nature.*

HB: Maybe it is. I think we have to look at what values-led change has to offer. Firstly, whose values are we talking about? We're looking at values identified by people themselves. We ask people: what is really important to you?

I believe in the spiritual world but there's no question we have lost out on that through formal and external adherence to religion. We don't reflect on things. Belief should come from within.

If you translate that into other areas, the deeper you go spiritually, the more honestly you look at human values. If you can make that journey you'll be more prepared to acknowledge and recognise the weakness of humanity.

My point is that the basis for this type of communitarianism is fallibility. We're all fallible. It's in acknowledging human weakness that you can build this kind of community.

As it is, scandals are being drawn out of institutions like teeth because society promoted the idea that institutions never make a mistake, a kind of infallibility. That those in power could never go wrong.

One immediate impact of communitarianism is to promote tolerance. Gradually we need to move towards understanding that the sacred is in the human person and that each person has all the weaknesses of the next. If we accept this, we get involved together in a search rather than expecting certitude and demanding compliance.

FS: *Where does this optimism come from?*

HB: The more people are allowed to participate in their own future, the more I think goodness will come out of them. I believe there's a basic goodness in people but by not allowing them to get involved or share they get entrenched in a dependency culture. It's always somebody else's fault when things go wrong. They get cynical. By allowing them to participate and by including people, you tap into a lot of the goodness that's in there.

Once you get people into structures that allow them to participate, I think there's a practical work programme for a model of community to do with parenting, the elderly, schooling, work practices, professions. This thing can only grow through debate, through identifying real issues.

It's an attitudinal change more than anything else. That will lead to the practical stuff but you're dealing with a mind-set first. When you think of it, it's not just this busy-ness that's keeping us from reflecting on where we are. We've become a media-dominated society and yet it's almost impossible to debate serious issues on current affairs programmes. So much of it is taken up with trivial stuff that does not reflect real life.

FS: *What makes you believe that people want to change the way things are?*

HB: I hear it and I see it. Some young people told me recently that they felt they were being forced to live a very superficial life. They felt if they expressed anything that is beyond the usual agenda of being cool such as sex/success/pastimes/pleasure/career/comfort, they are looked at as being different and strange. They were afraid to be different so it was easier to go with the flow.

It's fairly obvious that the debate itself is hugely important. What we're finding is that people from a cross-section of Irish society are coming forward in growing numbers to get involved in that debate.

So there's a momentum there. The starting point for us is to begin the search and research into where people are. As we move on to set up branches around the country, we'll get a better picture because it will involve committed people from corporate, community, religious, educational, public sector, professions, parenting, schooling and other sectors.

FS: *Where might this search and research go from there?*

HB: This diverse range of people will meet to discuss and identify where we are. I have found that we can get to the heart of these issues by considering what values are missing in modern Irish society. This is what we need to reflect on. What values do we need to restore or protect and how do we put them into practice?

That might seem a nice little cosy thing to be doing but it's not any more. The groups we set up through Céifin will identify values that have been overlooked by the speed and excesses of modern life. In other words, most people have a core set of values but the everyday pace of life has got so fast and so busy there's no space to reflect on them.

FS: *How does this translate into the application of new values?*

HB: Having participated in the process over a period of time, our aim is for individuals to introduce the same process into their workplaces, schools, churches, families, communities.

Once people begin to realise that, in taking time out to identify what is of real value in their lives, major change can take place at individual and organisational levels and of course eventually at the level of policy-making.

It's a huge challenge but it's no good taking time to reflect on serious issues if that doesn't lead to practical action. Freire's term "Praxis" is a word I've gotten very fond of — the process of reflecting upon one's world and of acting upon it to change it.

And equally, if we're going to have change we need to think about it fully before we start implementing anything.

The way I see it, change has to be values-led. These difficulties or complexities — whatever you want to call them — in modern life have been generated by change where nobody thought about the longer-term effects. Or where core values were chipped away and eroded. This is a way of restoring the balance. It's not the first time I've used that phrase, but it's what we're talking about.

If we're going to do that, we need to bring everybody into the debate. There's no point having one sector of society — say, religious, for example — deciding what values society is now lacking. We really want to promote the idea of a joint or partnership approach.

People are not going to stay compartmentalised. Society has become too complex for that, so a teacher can also be a parent, a professional, a city dweller as well. We're not just single category units and our research has to recognise that.

The partnership approach is the best way to proceed. It might seem a bit vague to be looking at the value of things, but you have to first establish basic principles and then move onto practicalities.

FS: *Can one person make a difference?*

HB: I don't know if it's possible for one person to achieve real changes — I'd like to think it is. If the dominance of the market continues it will get more difficult to do so. We are going to be forced to think about the other side of life, to form new types of communities, forced to look at these values and apply them. It will only be possible as real events continue to scream at us and tell us we have no choice except to change course.

That's why I feel we have to do a serious amount of research on what is happening to people out there. You have to put figures opposite a lot of the stuff that's happening, whether it's people dying on the roads or overdosing on drugs or whatever. And having done that, then ask questions. The way we have been addressing a lot of these questions — say, poverty for example — is through charitable organisations. The way these questions have to be addressed in the future is to get to the root cause and then put a different type of structure in place to address it.

FS: *What is to be gained from Céifin becoming a national organisation?*

HB: I would see it as a movement. Each branch will be bringing together people working in partnership to identify the issues they want addressed. They will then link into a national movement — people from Dundalk can share with people in Waterford and Cork and so on. Just as each branch covers different sectors, there is huge benefit from hearing what similar groups in other parts of the country are encountering on the ground.

The Céifin Institute will carry out a lot of research that will feed into these branches as well, providing them with back-up information on what they need to know. I would see this gathering momentum as a people's movement. This dynamic is not limited to Ireland either. There is a search going on and it's important that the people involved in it realise they're part of a worldwide movement.

What they have in common is that this all starts from where people are. The next step is to challenge institutions to respond.

In return, this has great potential to create a whole new approach by institutions. Instead of the established practice of handing down truths from on-high, institutions — including the Catholic Church — would have to be open and receptive to the concerns that people have. Rather than a top-down model, it's a two-way street.

FS: *Is there a perception of community or communitarianism as being a woolly "good life" idea. That it's nice, but in the real world, sort of anti-progress?*

HB: Yes. It's a soft word against a hard word like economy or technology. It might sound like a nebulous sort of thing, except all our studies are based on the real world.

In one survey of children at school, we found that seven out of ten children come home to an empty house every day. To me, the implications of that are enormous. Suppose three-quarters of children come home each day and are not able to tell their story. Later, when they are 15 or 16, they may not be able to confide in their parents — communication will have broken down. That's a communitarian issue that affects progress but it's not something that you'll find in statistics on workforce or employment levels.

In the past, a lot of serious damage was done to children who were put through industrial schools. What is the threat today? Who are we handing over responsibility to?

FS: *Is there more than a semantic difference between "soft" terms and "hard" terms?*

HB: I think so. It's as though the soft words don't need much attention and the hard words command respect. For example, you have a "hard" term like "market value" which belongs to the world of business. We need to re-consider these terms and what they mean, because if market values take over professions that serve people, then there are going to be problems. And I think that is already happening.

For example, we could say that market value has interfered with the profession of accounting. If the profession of accountancy no longer holds business to account for itself, inevitably it all goes wrong. We've had this on a massive scale with major American corporations this year and a few worldwide accountancy firms that were previously regarded as highly respectable organisations.

The same principle applies if market value becomes a part of health services. Only recently did the South African government challenge the patent owners for HIV and AIDS drugs. It is unacceptable to me that millions of people in Africa are dying because they can't afford these drugs. The market value dictates a high price for them, yet if the motive was compassion instead of profit, these drugs can be manufactured much more cheaply. That's what I'm talking about.

FS: *Where might human values fit into the money economy?*

HB: What I'm really saying is that market value is so central, so ingrained in people's thinking, we behave as though there isn't an alternative. We're not even thinking any other way any more. Yet we moan and moan about all the realities that confront us every day.

We've yet to come up with a wider strategy. But you can see where it's needed on the ground — for a start, let's propose that people who bring children into the world should be given the opportunity to rear them; or let's propose reforming the education system from being just the slave of the economy to becoming the servant of society.

Let's look at other areas. What about universities allowing students to take a year out to do public service? We're
constantly hearing that fewer and fewer people have any
time to give to the community. We have a good idea why
this is happening and we realise how potentially damaging it
is for society in general. But it's one thing knowing what the
situation is — doing something about it is another.

It applies across the board. Most people will complain
about traffic congestion these days, yet car-pooling has almost disappeared. Is this another problem that has to be
solved for us by somebody else?

The way I see it, this has to change. It's a question of all of
us taking responsibility, from the individual to the big corporation. It's just not enough for the corporate world to make a
small financial contribution to the local community and regard
this as fulfilling their social responsibility. The business world
has to get way more involved in the environment that it op-
erates in. It isn't enough just to hand out bits of charity.

I think it's beginning to sink in that the values that underpin life itself and give meaning to life have to be identified
and invested in. Prosperity is welcome over poverty, but
when society begins to worship at the shrine of mammon,
then the things which cannot be bought go into short supply.
We're talking about companionship, family happiness, friend-
ship, a sense of the sacred. Ironically, it's only when individuals, families and/or communities break down that we value
these things that money cannot buy.

There's a lot of work to be done in the area but if we
start thinking seriously about it, I believe there are solutions
to the problems we're facing. In a way, that's what Céifin is
all about. Maybe we should also remember that the problems we face also present opportunity for change.

FS: *You have just identified a 90-acre site four miles outside Newmarket-on-Fergus in County Clare to build the future Céifin Institute. What hopes do you have for the Institute?*

HB: The Céifin Institute will provide the hub for inspiring, informing and equipping people to deal with the issues which impact on their daily lives. It will provide a base for what we envisage as a communitarian movement.

We work on the basis that for effective communication the speaker must know the concerns of his or her listeners. In order to engage effectively with people regarding values and ethics, we must hear the experience of those we address. The message of human and spiritual values won't make any impact otherwise. It must use their language, it must answer the questions they ask and it must impact on their daily lives.

This could quickly transform society. Since we started this, I'm amazed at the general response. For example, we now have people coming from Church and State organisations to know if we can examine the future position of schools in relation to the community. If we hadn't started up this debate, they would be struggling with this problem, so I'm glad to say it's already showing results.

We are fast positioning ourselves to provide leadership forums to put ethics back into the centre of work practice and human relationships. We're also looking to provide a way forward for new models of community.

The Institute will provide a setting for professional, religious, corporate and community groups to spend time understanding change — both personal and organisational — and how they can engage in people-centred change in the future.

rote that you would like "*each individual [to] take
his or her sphere of influence rather than his or
cern*". What did you mean?

HB: I borrowed that from Stephen Covey, who stated it at one of our conferences. Effectively, it means we can all be concerned about issues — politics, Africa, global warming — but what we can influence is a different matter. It's a bit of a cop-out to get worked up over issues you can't do anything about and to ignore the things you can improve. To me, it's about challenging people to take social responsibility.

Through our annual conferences, Céifin has attempted to initiate debate around this issue. We began in 1998 by asking "Are We Forgetting Something?", dealing in subsequent years with "Working Towards Balance" and "Redefining Roles and Relationships". Last year we posed the question "Is the Future My Responsibility?"

If this is the way things are, do we all stand back and blame the institutions without taking responsibility ourselves? These are valid questions, but the answers aren't so simple. As a society we have got into this kind of confused world where we are debunking and blaming institutions and at the same time not taking any responsibility ourselves. At this year's conference — "Values and Ethics: Can I Make A Difference?" — we are proposing that people can make a difference if they take responsibility for their future — as far as possible.

FS: *If we are only breaking out of a long-established institutional system, is it asking a lot for everyone to start taking full responsibility?*

HB: I suppose it is and, of course, not everyone will get involved. But if we want a different kind of society, we must take the first steps and start investing intellectually and financially in this. For years we were totally dependent on Church and State to run our lives. The spectacular economic success of the '90s hastened a disconnecting from those institutions but I would argue that our new-found prosperity has merely switched that dependence to the corporation, the world of entertainment, the media and so on.

The freedom that came with breaking away from the past also began to provoke new and searching questions. I think we can put this in context because this new independence was accompanied by some instances of human diminution. For example, people in low-income groups or areas of social exclusion have not found things getting any better for them.

Other areas, particularly in the caring professions, also felt they were losing out. We see it in nursing, the health services generally, schooling. We know questions about this imbalance are not being answered because it's getting more difficult to recruit people to the public sector. That leads us certainly to wonder about the direction we are taking.

We need the opportunity to reflect. We, as individuals, have to challenge ourselves to play our part in ensuring that values and ethics play a central role in society and that the language of values is not lost.

More and more, the responsibility for providing the moral guidance, the ethical and inspirational leadership, will be down to each one of us. The debate is vital and so is the analysis but at the end of it, we must find practical solutions. We have to move from theory to practice. People are so caught up in the busy, noisy, confused world that it's easy to lose sight of the debate itself.

FS: *Maybe, as was suggested earlier, the issues seem so intractable that people feel it's too much to take on?*

HB: Sometimes I think it would be a lot easier to go out and make money than to address some of the ethical and moral issues to do with humanity. Even so, we have to get urgently involved in this debate because if we lose the understanding and appreciation of these values, the only values we'll have left would be money values.

In *The Third Wave*, Alvin Toffler coined the term "practopia" to describe a civilisation that's neither the best nor the worst of all possible worlds. A practical utopia. Sometimes I think of that when we get stuck in the debate between past and present but, like Toffler, I think that re-humanising society can give us something better than what we have.

It's very important that the debate is rigorous and relevant. The soft ethical stuff has to be tough and tested. You are into profound issues of justice and so on. People who get seriously involved in ethical issues have to believe deeply in them. They also need a lot of courage.

I do believe people are searching for these values. That's where we are now but we have a journey ahead of us. The people who are concerned about events out there, who are quite prepared to come to conferences and talk about them, have to be prepared to take the next step. The next step is not an easy one. It has to be about identifying these values and applying them.

FS: *In the course of our discussion, you have espoused particular concepts like values, ethics, communitarianism. In the context of where modern society stands, do traditional practices need to be reviewed to make them more relevant?*

HB: Well, we have to adapt our belief system to make it more relevant to how we live. One of the main changes in modern Ireland has been the decline of religion. This means simply that religion is no longer the uncontested centre and ruler of people's lives. The Catholic Church is no longer the final and unquestioned authority and we must accept that the Church and society are no longer the same thing.

The decline in the influence of religion marks a weakening of a whole system of symbols, images, ceremonies, dogmas and rights within which the whole of life had been safely contained. The fact that the Church is a partner in shaping society does make a difference.

Some people suggest that contemporary society is post-Christian. I don't believe this. There is still a deep longing in the hearts of people for a Christian response. However, it is clear that we are living at a critical time. If we come to lose our sense of right and wrong, we lose the very connection with the transcendent realm of our being.

People are set free to deal with this world in their own way. This is leaving a gap that is hard to fill, a "hole in the soul". This is a direct challenge to the Church to redefine its message.

More than anything, I think we as a society need to address that gap in a fruitful, thought-out way. We need to consider all the things we've raised here but if there's a parting thought, I'd like to underline the importance of community and soul.

Community is about relationships and the saving power of relationships to sustain us. It is not some abstract notion. It's about real people with real names. People in a community are not just "clients", "consumers" or "employees". They are all of these but they are, above all, people. Real community is characterised by interdependence in which the unique creativity of each person is a contribution to the other.

Which brings me, finally, to soul. Soul is part of every individual and of most communities and cultures. People from both the Eastern and Western traditions agree that the human form is sustained by mind, body and soul. If one of these elements is overlooked, the human form is in trouble. And when all three are nurtured, it sustains individuals, communities and the environment.

Soul is the existence of some kind of animating presence within humans and other living things. The ancient Hebrews called soul "Ruah" — the source of life. It also means breath or wind. The Maori peoples of New Zealand call it "Hau" — the life-giving spirit of the world. Soul is about deep meaning and quality of relationships. It is about mystery, the presence of something profound that cannot be grasped by science or the boundaries of human language. Soul balances the excesses of mind and body to sustain life. We need to nourish that.

Soul is about you and me. Soul is present in community in a lot of ways. As a society we make massive investments in nurturing the body and mind. Don't you think it's time we started nurturing the soul in the context of relationships and community?